the boy who would be a helicopter

By the same author

White Teacher (1979)

Wally's Stories (1981)

Boys and Girls:
Superheroes in the Doll Corner (1984)

Mollie Is Three:
Growing Up in School (1986)

Bad Guys Don't Have Birthdays:
Fantasy Play at Four (1988)

the boy
who would be
a helicopter

Vivian Gussin Paley

HARVARD UNIVERSITY PRESS

Cambridge, Massachusetts, and London, England 1990

For Danny, Michelle, and Debbie

This book is printed on acid-free paper, and its binding
materials have been chosen for strength and durability.

Library of Congress Cataloging-in-Publication Data

Paley, Vivian Gussin, 1929–
   The boy who would be a helicopter.

   1. Preschool teaching. 2. Teacher-student relationships.
3. Child development. 4. Fantasy in children—Case studies.
I. Title.
LB1140.3.P35   1990   372.11′02   89-24747
ISBN 0-674-08030-0 (alk. paper)

Designed by Gwen Frankfeldt

Contents

Foreword

ROBERT COLES

As I read through this extraordinarily touching and compelling account of a teacher's work with young boys and girls, of her work with younger teachers who are learning how to get on usefully and imaginatively with children, and not least of her work with herself—daring to stop and take stock, even acknowledge errors of opinion or judgment—I kept thinking of the last conversation I had with Anna Freud. She was in her eighties and had only four or five years of life left. She happened to be in a particularly retrospective mood that day; I heard her talk with special pleasure about her work during World War II with children who had suffered under the Nazi blitz, and her work shortly thereafter with those who had survived the Nazi death camps. We also discussed her long-standing difficulties with the psychoanalyst Melanie Klein, and in that regard Miss Freud was enlightening, as always, but now quite affecting and even humble, as she reflected on their different approaches:

> I have tried to let children take the initiatives [in her research], and to learn from them. Perhaps I might have deduced more from them than I did . . . I think if you put me in a room with young children . . . , you'd see me watching them carefully, trying to keep up with them in every way, and when I'd left them, you'd find me puzzling over what I saw and heard,

not too sure of myself, and even quite unsure. With
Mrs. Klein it was different, I suspect; I'm reasonably
sure she would have a pretty good idea (right away,
sometimes) what was happening with the children.
She was never reluctant to let us know that she had
a keen knowledge of the [psychological] lines of development in young children. A long time ago a colleague of mine asked me how [Mrs. Klein] knew so
exactly the moods of infants and pre-school children.
I was exasperated then; I remember saying: "Go ask
her, and come back and tell us!" Now, I would be
more relaxed; I'd say something like: "She knows
what we haven't yet found out, and so we should be
impressed." I'd probably add this: "Mrs. Klein has
told us what she believes happens to children, and
we're still trying to find out what does happen by
watching them and listening to them, and that's the
difference."

Miss Freud's attitude—that there is always more to learn
from children—is surely shared by Vivian Paley, who has
taught youngsters for many years and has for just as long been
their devoted, attentive student. This most recent of her books
shines with such a willing openness to new thoughts and ideas,
as they are prompted by the rush of events that take place in
the classroom. As she makes clear, for her a classroom is a
place where a constantly shifting and edifying series of en-
gagements takes place—between one child and another, between one "them" and another, between someone called an
adult, a teacher, and others called schoolchildren, and as we
learn in this book, between one adult who has been working
in schools for a long time and other adults who have less
experience. Most important for us, the readers, Vivian Paley is
a wonderfully lucid and appealing writer, a storyteller herself
who listens patiently and appreciatively to the stories of the
children she obviously gets to know exceedingly well. The
result is a captivating record of human encounters relayed to

us with candor and good sense—an important educational effort, and, too, an example of what the literary-documentary
tradition has to offer: an ongoing experience carefully recorded
and reported.

The special charm of this book is its real life quality—the
author's insistence that we come as close as possible to the
children she tried to know as well as possible. We meet them
as she did, as they speak out in their own various, inimitable
ways—one minute delightfully winning, the next quite confusing, even disturbing. We meet them as the storytellers they
are, as the actors and actresses they are, ever willing to perform
in plays written by themselves or others; and we meet them
because an imaginative teacher and a clear-headed writer is
willing to pay the closest heed and render what she has learned
in prose at once convincing and unprepossessing, a rare gift in
itself.

Needless to say, all readers will be especially interested in
Jason, "the boy who would [sometimes, at interesting moments, one hastens to add] be a helicopter." The book centers
on this interesting, provocative, inscrutable protagonist and
those who in one way or another want to comprehend him,
bring him out of himself, accommodate his ways with theirs.
It is an absorbing and by no means rare drama—the stubbornly
idiosyncratic outsider who yet captures the attention, if not the
interest and curiosity, of those inclined to find themselves comfortable with their neighbors in a particular community. Jason
gradually becomes Vivian Paley's teacher and, too, someone
who helps her teach other teachers, those who work with her,
and those who will read this book—many, I hope. I also hope
that all of us who do so, who meet an inspired teacher and her
lively young students, will remember how she has chosen to
present this book to us, with the emphasis on faithfully ren-
dered experience, so that generalizations and abstractions follow modestly. In an age when ambitious theorists strut across
any stage they can find, assaulting us with pronouncements
meant to advance careers, here is a teacher who lets life's
complexities have their full dignity, who moves ever so gently

and thoughtfully from observed life to carefully qualified comment, and who—surprisingly and refreshingly both—is quite willing to acknowledge error, to apologize to the children or her younger colleagues for mistakes made, to address her own blind spots. No doubt the young people whom we meet in the pages that follow knew how lucky they were to have such a teacher, just as the rest of us who get to know Vivian Paley through this book will be similarly grateful that she has written it.

Preface

Were someone to ask for a single example of my best teaching moment, I might give them Jason and the mother pig. The pig is in a story of Katie's, and Jason is the boy who tells us every day that his helicopter is broken.

"Come listen to Katie's story," I call to Jason. "This mother pig does something that reminds me of you."

He approaches the story table blowing on his blades, one of the many ways to repair a broken helicopter, and I read what Katie has just dictated to me.

> There is the three pigs. And the mother pig is there. Then the wolf huffs down the brick house. And the mother puts it back together.

"That makes me think of the way you fix your helicopter," I say.

Jason and Katie smile at each other, and I am a step closer to my vision of connecting everything that happens in this nursery school classroom. My habit of drawing invisible lines between the children's images is, I think, the best thing I do as a teacher, though Jason, whose story occupies most of this book, draws his own lines between himself and his helicopter.

He is, for me, the quintessential outsider, beyond race, place, or age. It is his self-defining image that separates him from us; he is the one we must learn to include in our school culture if it is to be an island of safety and sensibility for everyone. What happens to Jason in school is the mirror of its moral landscape.

There are labels that might be attached to Jason, but we'll neither define nor categorize him. None of us are to be found in sets of tasks or lists of attributes; we can be known only in the unfolding of our unique stories within the context of everyday events. We will listen to Jason's helicopter stories and offer our own in exchange. In this evolving classroom drama every revelation is necessary and equally important, for our goal is more than fantasy. It is fairness.

The story of Jason and his helicopter reminds us that every child enters the classroom in a vehicle propelled by that child alone, at a particular pace and for a particular purpose. Here is where the fair study of children begins and where teaching becomes a moral act.

Storytellers and

Story Players

"Who are you, Lilly?" I bend low to ask the bonneted figure pulling a straw purse over my feet.

"Me and Eli losted our baby," she says, disappearing into the cubby room.

Later, Lilly the story player becomes Lilly the storyteller, a fragile change of perspective that has enabled me, after many years, to find my role as teacher.

> Once upon a time the mother and the daddy goed
> hunting for their little girl. That girl is in a trapdoor.
> The end.

A day without storytelling is, for me, a disconnected day. The children at least have their play, but I cannot remember what is real to the children without their stories to anchor fantasy and purpose.

I listen to the stories three times: when they are dictated, when we act them out, and finally at home, as I transcribe them from my tape recorder. After that, I talk about them to the children whenever I can. The stories are at the center of this fantasy of mine that one day I will link together all the things we do and say in the classroom.

What if there had been no storytelling on the day Joseph needed to create a new ending for *Hot Hippo?* An angry ending. Then I could not have said to him on another angry day, "Remember when you were Hot Hippo and you ate up all the fish?"

In the original African tale, Hippo is hot. He goes to Ngai, god of all creatures, and asks to live in the water. No, says

Ngai, because you will eat my fish. I won't, promises Hippo: I'll swish my tail and open my mouth wide so you can see there are no fish bones. All right, says Ngai, but you must come out of the water at night. Hippo is content, and there the book ends.

But Joseph is compelled to reshape the issues. His Ngai commands Hippo to eat the fish. Joseph fairly rises from his seat as he speaks the words, "Jump in the water, Hot Hippo, and eat the fish! I hate them all. Eat up every animal!"

Samantha is not pleased. She decides to be Hippo in a story of her own. Now, when Hippo asks to live in the water, Ngai falls dead and Hippo is the new god. "Hippo is the god of the whole everyone," Samantha announces. "And no bothering is allowed."

Who are these people who dare to reinvent mythology? They are the children found in every classroom thinking up plot and dialogue without instruction. And, for the most part, without the teacher's awareness.

Amazingly, children are born knowing how to put every thought and feeling into story form. If they worry about being lost, they become the parents who search; if angry, they find a hot hippopotamus to impose his will upon the world. Even happiness has its plot and characters: "Pretend I'm the baby and you only love me and you don't talk on the telephone."

It is play, of course, but it is also story in action, just as storytelling is play put into narrative form. The distinctions are important to me because this story playing and storytelling has become the curriculum of any classroom in which I am the teacher. Somewhere in each fantasy is a lesson that promises to lead me to questions and commentary, allowing me to glimpse the universal themes that bind together the individual urgencies.

"Lilly, I'm thinking about that lost girl. Do the parents find her?"

"They goed in the wrong forest. There's a lion in there."

"A friendly lion?"

"A king. It was the wrong forest to look."

In my early teaching years I was in the wrong forest. I paid scant attention to the play and did not hear the stories, though once upon a time I must have also imagined such wondrous events.

Indeed, my strongest childhood memories are of the daily chase of good and bad guys on the playground. Was I part of it or did I only watch? Silently I replayed the dialogues during the school day, and a note I wrote to someone—or perhaps it was written to me—reappears in my mind even today. "Who will you be? Can we pretend sisters?"

Nothing else mattered, only the play. We acted out fear and friendship and called into being characters who would speak the lines; our contentment depended on the roles we created.

But we were careful not to reveal these secrets in the classroom lest Ngai withdraw his love and permission to swim in the cool water. Ngai did not like so many Hot Hippos wasting school time telling their private stories.

Luckily, a thousand Ngais cannot erase the storytelling instinct. It is always there waiting to be resurrected. Even as I retell Joseph's Ngai story, I am compelled to fashion my own, for storytelling is contagious and listening to the children's stories will rekindle the teacher's.

Once we push deeply into the collective imagination, it is easier to establish connections and build mythologies. The classroom that does not create its own legends has not traveled beneath the surface to where the living takes place.

The fantasies of any group form the basis of its culture; this is where we search for common ground. That which we have forgotten how to do, the children do best of all: They make up stories. Theirs may be the original model for the active, unrestricted examination of an idea.

"I heered robbers," Edward whispers. "I'll put them in jail."

"No, me," Eli argues.

"Not both. That's too many. One has to . . . not too many."

"Yeah, you be the dad police and I'm the big brother police."

"Two both police?"

"Not too many."

"That's just two. Two both a dad and a brother also."

No teacher could conjure up as good a lesson to explain "too many" and "both." Eli and Edward, using fantasy play, are able to visualize such abstractions from inside a story. In dramatizing a concept, the child finds the natural method for concentration and continuity and satisfies the intuitive belief in hidden meanings.

This is why play feels so good. Discovering and using the essence of any part of ourselves is the most euphoric experience of all. It opens the blocked passages and establishes new routes. Any approach to language and thought that eliminates dramatic play, and its underlying themes of friendship and safety lost and found, ignores the greatest incentive to the creative process.

Play and its necessary core of storytelling are the primary realities in the preschool and kindergarten, and they may well be the prototypes for imaginative endeavors throughout our lives. For younger students, however, it is not too much to claim that play contains the only set of circumstances understandable from beginning to end.

Think of it. Here are two dozen children in self-selected acting companies, each group performing a different drama, moving through one another's settings, proclaiming separate visions of life and death, inventing new purposes and plots, and no one ever inquires, "What's going on?"

As Lilly dictates her story, half a dozen other themes splash noisily around us from all directions:

"Y'wanna play tiger? Sabre tooth?"

"Superman! I shotted you."

"Wah, wah, mommy, mommy!"

"Ghostbusters! Green Slimer!"

"Meow, meow, nice kitty."

"Are you the dad, Simon? Here's our cave for good bears."

Not one child asks, "What's everyone doing? Who are these crawling, crouching, climbing people?" There is no confusion, only the desire to fit into someone's story or convince a classmate to enter yours.

But let the teacher order so simple a change in routine as new snack groups, and the tension mounts. Whose group am I in? Where should I go? The teacher is not at fault. The natural order in a preschool classroom rules against any plan that sidesteps fantasy or friendship. The children do not fathom her premises or follow her logic.

Had the teacher said, "Simon, since you were Joseph's dad before in the bear cave, you must move to his table," then everyone would understand and approve. Or, had a child suggested, "Pretend a robber stealed the table and then we finded a different one," the new plan would come alive.

"Pretend" often confuses the adult, but it is the child's real and serious world, the stage upon which any identity is possible and secret thoughts can be safely revealed.

The great writers know this truth, remembering it from childhood. They depict characters who feel real only when pretending to be someone else. Deprived of illusions, they wander about asking, "Who am I? What should I be doing?"

And so too the children, newly arrived in school, drift and worry until someone shares a fantasy and there are roles to play. Then there comes a sense of place and person, and the words flow with purpose and pleasure.

If I am to step to the rhythm of the storytellers who inhabit my classroom, I must perform on their stage or we will seldom hear one another out. I can never, of course, be as they are, for a child storyteller is a story player.

Play is the model and play is the goal. The most rudimentary story told by a three-year-old, a mere listing of items on the table, has an unspoken plot.

"A crayon comes, a paper, a scissors" may be taken as: Pretend I am a crayon and I color on a paper and the scissors tries to cut me and I roll off the table.

There is always a plot. The words are imagined in action and they become the script for play. Samantha, age four, cuts out a circle and rolls it back and forth along the rim of the table as she waits for her turn to tell a story.

> Once upon a time there was a little baby who had a
> circle. And then she cried for her bottle. And then
> the circle was magic. And then when she cried she
> never cried again. She was a big girl.

The circle may indeed be magic, for how else could such a story appear? And Joseph's superhero play turns into a story just as easily. "I'm Batman!" he shouts, twirling his cape around between the tables.

"Why don't you be He-Man?" Alex says. "He's stronger."

"But I can fly. Watch my cape!"

Moments later, Joseph tells a story: "Once He-Man came and Batman flied higher. He was stronger. He saved the day."

"How did he save the day?" I ask.

"Because he trapped the bad guys," Joseph replies. "Hey, Alex, who do you want to be in my story?"

"Call me Skeletor."

This pleases Joseph, who confides, "Alex always rathers to be a bad guy." Joseph knows Alex's feelings about good and bad better than I do because they play together, and play is the most compelling and informative of all storytelling.

Fantasy play and storytelling are never far apart. Listen to Edward as we act out a story he has dictated. Before I can read many lines, he reverts to fantasy play. "You didn't say about the bad guy. And there's a wolf in there. Because there's a chimney. And a baby was there too."

Remarkably, each child's first story is a unique event in the history of the world. Lilly begins her storytelling career in a way neither I nor anyone else has ever heard before.

> The daddy turned off the television.

That is her story, nothing more. Her second story, two days later, brings in another event.

> Lilly didn't want to take off her pajama shirt. That's what I want to say.

After a week, a babysitter enters her story.

> Mashie. There was Mashie. She has black hair. And Mommy and Daddy. And Lilly.

The next story sounds almost the same, with one urgent addition.

> There was Mashie. And there was Mommy and Daddy. And there was Lilly. And the mommy stays.

By the end of the month, the effects of society and magic can be seen.

> There was a monster. He's not bad. And Katie is the mother. We need a baby. We need a daddy too. That's Edward. And he weared a tie. I'm the little girl with a cape. And she goed somewhere.

Lilly's stories have a new purpose: to leave behind the other real world and invent disguises that promise more control. Her stories will now resemble play, that most ordinary of human functions, as natural as crawling, walking, and running. Without instruction, these skills flourish. No one is taught to walk—or to act out a fantasy. The patterns and incentives arise from within.

Children pay no attention to the way they walk; they would stumble and fall if they continually observed themselves moving along. The effect would be worse if they watched everyone else as well.

Nor do children reflect upon their private fantasies; they are surprised and embarrassed if references are made to anything overheard when they are in this dream-like state.

The moment several children combine their imaginings, however, group instinct mandates a more conscious organization.

Now the children insist upon rules, demanding of one another intense concentration, contemplation, comparison, interpretation, and self-evaluation. Characterizations must ring true, and scenes are required to look and sound authentic if they are to reach the magical proportions that inform and protect the players.

The fact that all children share this view of play makes play, along with its alter ego, storytelling and acting, the universal learning medium. Children, at all ages, expect fantasy to generate—indeed they cannot stop it from doing so—an ongoing dialogue to which they bring a broad range of intellectual and emotional knowledge at a very early age.

Listen to ourselves as we leave the theater. Often we reach our most eloquent heights talking about what we have just seen, even if the movie or play is mediocre. Children's play and storytelling, by the way, are never off the mark to another child. So in tune are the young with each other's intentions that almost any story contains elements of truth.

Even "a crayon comes, a paper, a scissors"? Even that, for what more explicit representation of adult expectations greets the child upon entering the classroom than the tools of writing. It is the children who teach us the meaning of our symbols and rituals, making sense of them by pretending they are something else.

Children's own rites and images seem mainly concerned with the uses of friendship and fantasy to avoid fear and loneliness and to establish a comfortable relationship with people and events. In play, the child says, "I can *do* this well; I can *be* this effectively; I *understand* what is happening to me and to the other children."

In storytelling a child says, "This is how I interpret and translate right now something that is on my mind." Joseph puts aside his usual Batman or snake stories to tell a very different sort of story the day after his baby sister is born.

> Once upon a time there was a forest. And then there was a husband came. And a wife to the husband.

And a baby was there. And the baby had a gun.
And when the baby grew up the baby went hunting
with the father.

From where do such stories originate? One can imagine possible meanings: The forest represents the unknown; to call
mother and father a "wife and husband" shows Joseph's feeling
of estrangement; the baby with a gun—babies never have
guns—ensures its separation from the mother. There are no
certainties and no answers. Joseph has envisioned a story in
which to place his confusion. Having told his story and acted
it out, he knows something he did not know before, and he
will use the new information as the need arises.

For me the questions are: How can each day's priorities and
attachments be used to further an environment in which children tell us what they think? And what happens to those who
remain on the outside?

Jason is such a child. He speaks only of helicopters and
broken blades, and he appears indifferent to the play and stories that surround him. He has his own design for learning
and, so far, it seems different from everyone else's.

This makes Jason a valuable class member and an important
character in a book about teaching, for one does not teach in
the abstract. A style of teaching is best illuminated by those
who do not meet the teacher's expectations. These are the
children who shed the strongest light upon the classroom and,
this year, Jason carries the beacon, fastening it determinedly to
the inside of his helicopter house. He presents a vivid image,
but how do I mark his growth?

The proof of his progress may be in the list I keep of the
words and phrases he learns to borrow from the children who
push their way into his private world. Yet why should this
discovery surprise me? Have I not said and written over and
over that this is what is supposed to happen?

I have said as much but apparently have not entirely understood or believed in the process until Jason comes along and

shows me how it works when it doesn't appear to be working. As I learn to listen to what he tells us about his helicopter fantasy, I begin to see in new ways that only by reaching into the endemic imagery of each child can we proceed together in any mutual enterprise. All else is superficial; we will not have touched one another.

Before I tell Jason's story, there is more to say about my own. The teachers are included in this community of storytellers; the children show us that every story in the classroom influences all the others and must be told.

Teacher and
Theory-Maker

I was neither a good listener nor an able storyteller when my name became Teacher. What I doubtless knew as a child was buried under piles of disconnected information. I was a stranger in the classroom, grown distant from the thinking of children.

I knew myself no better than I did the children. How was I to behave? How could I know what to say to so many children when I could hardly recall anything a teacher ever said to me? Paradoxically, as the focus shifted from me to the children—what does it mean to be a child and what do children think about in the classroom?—I began to see my own role more clearly.

A graduate student named Fritz helped me begin to listen to the children. He wondered about the accuracy of a teacher's perceptions and, among other things, he proved to me that a boy named Charles was not a villain disguised as a five-year-old.

"Charles, you're grabbing all the sand!" I cry, rushing to defend his classmate.

"He don't mind. I need it."

"But that pile is in front of Tommy. You didn't ask him."

"He knows that's where the castle hasta be."

Charles is the biggest troublemaker, I complained, but Fritz's charts revealed otherwise. Charles, in fact, was a leader in non-aggressive play 80 percent of the time. Apparently, *I* was the troublemaker: 75 percent of my comments to Charles were negative.

None of this surprised Fritz, who measured and charted each

day the amount of time I believed Charles was misbehaving and the reality of the case. Fritz was accustomed to such large variances, but I was distraught. Pitying me, Fritz offered charts with which to improve my behavior, the goal being an 85 percent positive response. Obediently, I kept an eye on the clock, said good things to Charles, and checked off the daily columns.

The chart-keeping lasted only a week but was not without value. As with nearly all the research I encounter, it made me observe the scene more closely. Listening to Charles in order to compliment him, I heard the reasons for his classmates' esteem. He provided them with an unending supply of characters and plots.

"Hey, Tom, y'wanna play castle? This is a drawbridge."

"I got the key for it."

"You can't. There wasn't no keys invented yet. This is the only place keys can go. Okay, put it there. It's a fighting spaceship. It can kill someone by its power. Hurry up, pull up the drawbridge. The invisible bees is here. Quick, get your magic key. Pretend this is magic. Touch it and we turn into dragons!"

I measured my resistance against the children's eagerness and wondered what I was missing. And, since *I* was now doing the wondering—not Fritz—the matter was destined to reach larger proportions. Until I had my own questions to ask, my own set of events to watch, and my own ways of combining all of these with teaching, I did not learn very much at all.

Charts were not my way; this had been true also when I was a schoolchild, but I had forgotten. And even Piaget—whose experiments I repeated for three years and whose every word about children seemed remarkable and true—even Piaget could not direct me to take my own next step or prepare me for discussions such as the following.

"We must talk about cleanup," I say one day at rug time. "I have a complaint. Too many children are not helping. Some of you go into the book room instead of doing a job."

"You could put a trap door," Joseph says.

"I'm serious, Joseph. We're not talking about trap doors. I'm talking about people who don't help clean up."

"Lock them in," Samantha offers. "Then they'll be locked up."

"A trap door is better," Joseph insists. "See, if they're in there at cleanup time, it would fly open and trap them."

"Someone could get hurt," I say.

"I agree with Joseph," Simon shouts. "Then they fall where the cleanup job is."

"Yeah, yeah, a trap door is great," Alex joins in. "It's a slide so they don't fall. They slide up to the job."

"What if they fall back down? I think locking is better," Arlene says.

"Yeah, because I could find the key."

The discussion has galloped away from me. Once a magical solution is suggested there is no way to bring the children back. But I try. "I don't care for the idea of a trap door. Let's figure out some new rules."

"Get a guard," Simon says.

"With a gun!"

"No shooting, right, teacher?" Samantha is determined to be reasonable. "Okay. A trap door then," she concludes.

Joseph's trap-door image hovers over us, and my notion of reality is overwhelmed by the children's desire to place the problem in a fantastical setting. They do not pretend to be storytellers; they *are* storytellers. It is their intuitive approach to all occasions. It is the way they think.

For a while, cleanup *is* better; people always are more agreeable and generous after a good talk. In this case, the children prefer to imagine armed guards and trap doors as more sensible reasons for our endless cleanup chores. *It makes for a better story.*

We were taught to say that play is the work of children. But, watching and listening to them, I saw that play was nothing less than Truth and Life.

In moving from the glib acceptance of play to a serious analysis of its content, I have studied the subject through teaching and writing, and I cannot do one without the other. For me, the tape recorder is a necessity. I transcribe each day's play and stories and conversations and then make up my own stories about what is happening. The next morning my reality will be measured alongside the children's.

As with play itself, the process is never ending. The children invent new images and symbols every year, and I continually expand my definitions of what we are doing in the classroom.

There was a time when I believed it was my task to show the children how to solve their problems. I wrote: I do not ask you to stop thinking about play. Our contract reads more like this: If you will keep trying to explain yourselves, I will keep showing you how to think about the problems you need to solve.

After a few years, the contract needed to be rewritten: Let me study your play and figure out how *play* helps you solve your problems. Play contains your questions, and I must know what questions you are asking before mine will be useful.

Even this is not accurate enough. Today I would add: Put your play into formal narratives, and I will help you and your classmates listen to one another. In this way you will build a literature of images and themes, of beginnings and endings, of references and allusions. You must invent your own literature if you are to connect your ideas to the ideas of others.

Three-year-old Vinnie hugs her teddy bear upside down and tells her first story:

There was a bear that he standed on his head.

Acted out, the one-sentence story provides a strong role for Vinnie. She has contributed to the literature and culture of a previously unknown group of children. Now she is known, and soon she will know others through their stories, those revealed in play and those made permanent on paper.

The stories are literature; the play is life. From the start, all roads led to fantasy play, but my maps were poorly drawn. I agonized and intellectualized while the children played out solutions to their immediate problems and distant fears.

When Sylvia, a "problem" child of long ago, cried and kicked in a doll-corner crib and then began to dump the dishes on the floor, I worried that she was disrupting the other girls' play. When the girls forced her to change her behavior, it almost seemed that the fantasy play was a primitive form of behavior modification designed to alter the actions of bothersome classmates.

I was wrong. The out-of-step child, I discovered none too soon, is out-of-step only according to my rhythm. In the children's view, Sylvia was acting out one of the many roles available in a family drama.

She did not spoil the play. If Sylvia had not been "bad baby," someone else would have had to take the role. "Bad baby" and, for that matter, "angry mother" or "mean sister" are basic themes in the spontaneous theater of the young.

Once I began to view the children as storytellers and playwrights, the potential of fantasy as a learning tool overwhelmed my conventional expectations for the classroom.

Such is the way life in the classroom reinterprets the research. Whatever else I may choose to watch and record, my subjects draw me into deeper concerns and more vivid visions of their world. This would also be true if I were following the children's reading or math skills, but, when fantasy is the game—as it might well be in reading and math— the connections are more complex and subtle.

Fantasy is a boundless topic that submits to no labels. Do we adults not continue to wonder about and, in a sense, research our own fantasies all of our lives? Was it not my own best-beloved teacher fantasy that led me to worry over every inch of the classroom in pursuit of the yellow brick road on which the children and I would skip along to a magical kingdom?

And the fantasy of being able to explain how it truly is with children made me finally try to separate the distractions from the real thing and stop to listen to the children. Their fantasies propelled me further into surprises and mysteries, and I hungered after better ways to report what I heard and saw, and to find out what it all had to do with teaching.

This is not too much to expect from fantasy. The children do the same thing every day without benefit of a tape recorder and we call it play. They transcribe and expose the words and images that crowd their minds and place them on a stage, becoming actor, writer, critic, linguist, mathematician, and philosopher all at once. And they do not need us to teach them how.

I do, however, need them to teach me what fantasy is meant to do, and nearly everything I want to think about and write about makes better sense turned into a story. All the more so as the storytellers I now listen to are just beginning their school careers.

They take nothing for granted; everything is eventually put into a story. After more than thirty years of teaching, I must still listen carefully if I am to understand how complex ideas are studied in play. No theme is too convoluted to be unraveled by the powers of make-believe.

Katie, Simon, Alex, and Arlene are playing "waterbed." I have been hearing their meowing—they are four cats in a spaceship—but, as I tune in, it becomes clear that "waterbed" is the topic.

"Where do I sleep?" Simon asks.

"In the waterbed because you're the dad."

"The water turned into a bed?"

"Turn the bed so it won't squeak."

"And leak. Squeak and leak. And peek."

"Only dads and moms can peek there."

"Meow! The water's coming down!"

"Help! Help! We can't swim. A monster!"

"In the water he is."

"The bed's in the waterbed!"

"Here's the floaters, jump in the floaters."

Later, Simon tells this story:

Once there was a little squirrel. And his mother said,
"Go sleep in a waterbed." So he did. And he
drownded inside. And he got not-drownded because
it leaked out and he leaked out. The mother told him
to swim home. But he couldn't swim.

"How does the little squirrel get home, Simon?" I ask. "Since
he can't swim."

"It wasn't a ocean. It was just a stream. So he walked home."

The play and the stories and the talk nourish one another
and translate into ever more logical thought and social effectiveness. It is all there—this original intellectual and emotional
energy—a garden waiting to burst into flower.

Today, Joseph has brought a toy snake to school. "Put me
on the story list," he announces, in lieu of saying hello.
"There's a snake in my story."

Joseph's greeting is not unusual. The list he refers to is taped
to the large round table we call the story table, though it looks
like any other messy classroom depository of crayons, markers,
paper, scissors, and paste. Here sit the storytellers, picture
makers, and paper cutters, watching, listening, and sounding
forth as so many characters in a Saroyan play. Nearly everyone
has something to say to the storyteller.

The effect, by the way, is quite different when the dictation
takes place at a private corner desk or out in the hallway. Our
kind of storytelling is a social phenomenon, intended to flow
through all other activities and provide the widest opportunity
for a communal response. Stories are not private affairs; the
individual imagination plays host to all the stimulation in the
environment and causes ripples of ideas to encircle the lis-
teners.

My role in the process is made clear from the start: First, I
enable others to hear the storyteller by repeating each sentence
as I write it down. This also gives the storyteller a chance to
correct me if I am in error, or to change the contents of the
story if another idea comes to mind.

"There's not one witch. There hasta was two witches," Arlene tells me.

"And is there one cat? You said 'Comes the cat.'"

"Katie is one cat and Lilly is a mother cat. That's two cats. Because there hasta have a mother because of that."

"Ah, because of the witches? When there are witches there must be a mother?"

"Yes."

I question any aspect of the story I might misinterpret—any word, phrase, sound effect, character, or action that does not make sense to me without further explanation. The child knows the story will soon be acted out and the actors will need clear directions. The story must make sense to everyone: actors, audience, and narrator.

"Yaaah! They falled in a trap!"

"Who did? The witches?"

"No, there is a bad guy in the trap."

"So there is another bad guy besides the witches?"

"These are good witches." Arlene decides to play it safe.

The child's purposes and mine are closer together in this activity than any other I know of in the classroom. We both want to talk about the stories, a fact that lends credence to my third role as connection-maker. Throughout the day I may refer to similarities between a child's story and other stories, books, or events, though I try to avoid doing this while the story is being dictated. I don't wish to impose undue influence on the course of the story. The children, of course, have no such qualms; influencing one another is exactly what they intend to do.

Katie is first on today's list. "There's a snake in my story too," she tells Joseph, though a moment earlier we had been informed that her story was about a red crayon. "A red crayon comes," she had begun, but now her goal is to capture Joseph's attention.

"Once upon a time a snake comes," she says, and Joseph

and Simon sit down to listen. "And then a lion scardered them away."

"Who is them?" I ask.

"Yeah, who's them?" echoes Simon. The children copy my habit of questioning the storyteller, hardly needing me to instruct them. They question one another continually in play and I simply do as they do. I have, in fact, learned from them about question asking. They seldom, for instance, ask a question of another child if they already know the answer.

"Is there someone in the story besides snake, Katie?"

"It's alligator!" She is surprised. Don't I remember that Simon was alligator in a recent story of Joseph's?

"Don't have a bad alligator," Simon tells her.

"I won't."

In storytelling, as in play, the social interactions we call interruptions usually improve the narrative. Yet I can recall a time when I would say, "Please don't interrupt. Let people tell their own stories." That was when I missed the main point of storytelling. I did not understand it to be a shared process, a primary cultural institution, *the social art of language.*

Katie continues: "And then came the mother." There is always a mother in Katie's story. It is her main theme; all else is stage business and socializing. "I'm the mother," she says. "I growed big and I scardered the lion away by a red crayon."

"*Scared* the lion?" I offer to correct.

"Scar-der-rered," she insists and is off to the doll corner before I can ask why the lion is afraid of a red crayon.

Perhaps I'll find out later when we act out her story. It is one of my favorite kinds of questions because there is no way to anticipate the answer. Sometimes I wonder if the children deliberately think up such oddities because they know it pleases me to find good questions. Even if this could be true, it would demonstrate that children feel rewarded by the genuine curiosity of others. In an environment where people listen carefully and ask relevant questions because they need more information, storytellers may indeed be inspired to put surprises into their stories. Inevitably, the children learn the logical implications of an unexpected outcome. It is good training for the lifelong study of cause and effect.

Joseph hands his snake to Simon. "I got to do my story. Make him a big house and a front door and a back one to hide."

Now we'll see parallel stories in production: Joseph's at the story table and Simon's in the blocks. There will be several interpretations of snake and alligator today; the theme is in the air. And those variations that reach the printed page will themselves be expanded and altered once they are acted out.

Long ago I discovered that the dictated segment represents but a moment in a story's life. After we act her story, Katie adds, "And the baby cries."

"The baby?"

"You didn't see her because she's small."

Katie's story is a living, evolving entity, influenced by the drama around her as well as the one inside. Joseph puts his snake on the table and it becomes a character in her story; the red crayon with which she absentmindedly draws rainbow arcs is used to scare the lion; if Arlene sits beside her in the story room, then a little sister may be included. No, I forgot: Arlene no longer accepts *little* roles. She is a big sister, teenager, or mother.

When storytelling becomes playwriting, children are even more sensitive to the preferences of others. Joseph, now in his second year of storytelling, often consults with his actors as he develops a story.

> Once when snake was sleeping and he was hearing noises bump bump bump that was his friend alligator. That's Simon. Then there was a bang dong ding dong. Do you like that, Simon? And then snake said to alligator, "I want something to eat," and alligator said, "Come to my house." Then the mother snake comes. Katie, you're the mother snake. And she has six babies. Then a lion comes and the lion tries to get into the dream but he can't. So he goes away.

"How does the lion try to get into the dream?" I ask.

"He goes gr-r-r and he pushes with his feet on the white part."

"Does snake hear him?"

"No, because he sleeped tight."

Dreams are an expansive topic in general, and a dream that enters a story offers endless possibilities for the curious teacher.

"Remember we talked about how the lion tries to get into the dream?" I ask Joseph when we act out his story. Of course he remembers. Children remember every event connected to their stories and play. Joseph reproduces his answer verbatim. He doesn't need a tape recorder, as I do, to keep an accurate record.

Immediately, Alex has advice for Joseph. "Pretend the lion went inside the dream and when he seed so much of snakes he goes wha-a-ah! and he runs away." Alex, as the lion, has enlarged his own role, just as he would do in play. Intuitively the children perceive that stories belong in the category of play, freewheeling scripts that always benefit from spontaneous improvisations.

Stories that are not acted out are fleeting dreams: private fantasies, disconnected and unexamined. If in the press of a busy day I am tempted to shorten the process by only reading the stories aloud and skipping the dramatizations, the children object.

They say, "But we haven't *done* the story!" It is the same complaint we hear when the cleanup bell sounds. "We didn't get to play in the spaceship yet. We only just builded it!" The unacted story has not been played in; it is an empty structure. The process is incomplete.

The children like to dramatize books and fairy tales but are not dismayed if there is time only to read them. Acting them out is better, but listening is usually enough. They feel quite differently about their own stories. Once they see them in action, they are never again satisfied with half-a-loaf.

Furthermore, from the teacher's point of view, the events of play and story form the children's best subject, the one they are most eager to discuss and extend to other issues.

"I'm still thinking about that lion and the dream," I tell Joseph at snack. "You said the lion couldn't get into the dream because the snakes were asleep."

"Yeah, see, when you stay sleeping the gate locks."

"The gate to the dream?"

"Both gates, right, Joseph?" Simon calls out. "Front and back, right?"

"Yeah. But Joseph," Alex says excitedly, "sometimes a bad guy that kind of dragon with that dark part could get in because he walks where the rug doesn't come."

"Then you hear the footsteps?" I ask. "Because there's no rug?"

"Yeah, like in my kitchen. I hear dinosaurs those kind of dinosaur steps that are huge." Alex has everyone's attention.

"Make a trap," Joseph decides. "Then he goes whoosh down to the hole to the dungeon."

"Say, Joseph, I wonder if Katie's red crayon could scare the lion in that dream," I suggest.

"Uh-uh. That kind is not for dreams." By which he must mean: Dreams cannot be controlled by other people's magic. "But you could use it for a story," he adds graciously.

These are open-ended dialogues. Since the children invent the premises, they can push further and further toward the logical consequences of their positions. They easily debate such questions as: What happens in a dream? What sort of magic protects the dreaming child? Does the fact that you can imagine different endings to a story mean that you have more control over a story than you do over a dream? But if you tell a story *about* a dream, what sort of control is that?

Here are the serious and lively issues that enter the literature and lore of the classroom, but Jason is not yet curious enough to listen. His attention is cornered by his helicopter. "This blade is turning around faster faster faster oh no! now it's broken oh broken I have to fix it!"

Jason's Story

We watch Jason as he crouches behind the arrangement of blocks he calls an airport. The children are learning his monologues by heart. "This blade is turning around now you're going faster now you're going faster now you're going to crash now you're going off the ground now you're going up up up now you're going loud br-r-r-roooom now you're going to land pshshsh okay all safely."

The children are curious about this dark-haired boy and his helicopter fantasy, though he will not play with them or respond to their questions. But they are impressed by infatuations; they admire strong feelings openly displayed in extravagant shapes and sounds.

"We're flying past O'Hare," Jason says to his helicopter. "And we're flying past Midway and then we're flying to England. And then past England to O'Hare and then past O'Hare to Midway. And then the plane lands there. And then the propeller stops. Oooo-ooo it's spinning so fast!"

They keep track of Jason's private spectacle while I worry about that which does not take place. He plays alone; he tells stories to himself; he seems unaware of our habits and customs. Ask him a question and he says his helicopter is broken. Suggest an activity and he rushes away to fix his helicopter, sometimes knocking over a building in his path.

Some intuition tells Jason he must oppose our purposes and protect himself from our intrusions. He wails in fright if his helicopter is touched, and he breaks up our talk with ear-splitting noises. Appearing to push us away, he achieves the opposite: We cannot take our eyes off him.

One day when Jason is not in school, I tell a story to the small group that sits at his snack table.

"There was once a boy who would not say hello to anyone, not even to the teacher."

"Is it a true story?" Lilly asks.

"I'll tell some more and you can decide. Instead of hello he said 'Br-r-room!' Every day he roared as he walked past the teacher on his way to the blocks."

"'Good morning!' the teacher would call out. 'You brought your red helicopter today!'"

The children smile in recognition. "Is it Jason?"

"I'll tell more. The boy did not answer the teacher. He was busy carrying big blocks to a corner by the window."

"It's Jason, I know, I know," Alex beams. "You're just pretending a story, right?"

"Yeah, yeah," they all tell me. "It's just pretend. That's really Jason."

The children are pleased with my story; they see nothing wrong with someone saying, "Br-r-room!" instead of hello.

"Is the story finished?" Lilly asks.

"One more part. Then the boy landed his helicopter in the airport. And when it landed something happened."

"The blades got broken!" everyone yells happily. "And he fixed them!"

"That's the end." My story is done, and I've found out what I need to know. Jason's story makes sense to the children. It is up to me to discover why.

"Tell it again," Joseph says.

"I will when Jason is here. Do you think he'll like to hear it?"

"Of course he will," Lilly assures me. "It's about his helicopter."

The day Joseph brings a snake and tells a snake story, I say to Jason, "Come look at Joseph's snake. It moves in a funny way."

But Jason rushes past us into the blocks, his lips sputtering as he builds his first airport of the day. It will be dismantled and reconstructed many times. Breaking and fixing is Jason's design for play.

Joseph ends his story and calls to Simon, "Hey, pretend a bad alligator creeped downstairs, okay?" He sounds as if he is beginning a new chapter in the story he just dictated.

"Yeah, and then we hiss him? Then we fighted him," Simon says.

"Aren't you the alligator?" Joseph asks.

"I'm a baby squirrel that changed to a snake. Hi, dad. Are you the dad? I'll be the child, okay? The snake-friend-child and person that changes to a snake." The question of identity is every child's most serious preoccupation. To the two snakes in the snake house, nothing is more important.

Joseph grabs the nearest block and holds it up. "I'm the dad that has a sword and a key. But who's the alligator? Hey, Jason, you're the alligator, okay, Jason?"

Jason inches down behind the blocks. "This blade is turning around," he murmurs. "Now you're going up up up down down down oh you're going to crash broken you're broken I have to fix this blade now."

"Jason, look at me!" Simon yells. "Y'wanna be a alligator or not? A good alligator?"

"This is a rescue helicopter," Jason says louder, but not to the boys who shout his name. "Someone broke it. I have to fix the blades."

Joseph persists. "I gotta idea, Jason. Your helicopter hasta rescue us, okay? Help, help! A monster alligator in the dark! Save me! Helicopter to the rescue! Save the day!"

Joseph glares at the silent boy bent over a helicopter. His best logic will not work, and he is puzzled. So am I. The function of classroom fantasy, as both Joseph and I see it, is to communicate ideas and influence group culture. But Jason's play seems to have a different goal. He wants us to know his helicopter story, yet we are not to enter its sphere. How reliable can my theories be if they do not include Jason?

It is helpful, therefore, for me to change from theory-maker to storyteller if I am to follow the classroom lives of children who do not assume expected roles. A storyteller, above all, likes suspense. It is the *not* knowing about characters that makes them interesting. In a good story we watch for the unanticipated turn in the plot, and we presuppose that we are not seeing the entire picture.

Jason's ritual of broken blades and comforting repairs is as interesting a beginning to any child's story as I have heard. We wait for developments but so far Jason prefers to elaborate on the beginnings of his story.

The boys turn from Jason and arrange a row of wooden cylinders on the walls of the snake house. "Pretend this is poison drinks but the alligator doesn't know it's poison and he dies and he's dead."

"Pretend we put it in the helicopter . . ." Simon glances hopefully at Jason but there is no response. The children offer him new roles, but he will not step out of the one he knows.

Uninvited, I enter the scene. "I heard Joseph call for help, Jason. Can your helicopter save the snakes?"

Jason will not be manipulated by me. "My blade is broken," he says. "Someone broke this blade."

"Can you show Joseph and Simon how you fix it?"

"I can't show someone how you fix it."

He calls the children "someone." After two months, he refers to no one but me by name. Nonetheless, Jason's modus operandi is a story—of broken blades and power regained—and our curriculum is based on storytelling. We need only to tempt him onto one of our stages.

I have discovered something important about children. Anything that happens during their play or storytelling makes for captivating conversation as long as I am sincere. It is the fascination actors and playwrights have for constructive responses from the audience. When Lilly told me Jason would like my story about him, she based her opinion on this premise.

At snack time, I say, "An interesting thing happened in the blocks before to Joseph, Simon, and Jason." This *is* sincere because I did find it interesting. The children sit up at attention.

Even Jason is curious about a recollection in which he is seen as a central character.

"Joseph and Simon were snakes and there was a bad alligator and Simon wanted Jason's helicopter to save the day and . . ."

"No, *I* said to save the day," Joseph corrects me.

"Oh, yes, but Jason was busy fixing his helicopter blades because someone broke them."

"Who?" several children ask.

"I don't know," I say.

"Who broke your blades?" Joseph inquires with renewed interest.

"Someone who is orange," Jason whispers.

Joseph inspects his own orange shirt. "You mean someone who has on a shirt like this? But not me, right? You mean someone else that was orange?"

"He means a ghost that was orange!" Petey explodes, pounding the table. "Dum-de-dum-dum!"

Jason has heard enough talk. Lips pressed together, he emits a siren-like scream and whirls into the next room. He crashes through an elaborate web of train tracks and falls over an outraged Edward. "You did it on purpose!"

But Jason is already nestled behind his wall fixing his helicopter, not listening.

What makes children pay attention to the ideas and demands and complaints of classmates? The same conditions, I think, that create sense and order of other classroom enigmas: the need to have a friend and be part of a dramatic structure. Children see themselves, always, inside a story. Indeed, friendship itself is defined in terms of fantasy roles. You are a friend if you take part in someone's play, and you are most likely to listen to those with whom you are acting out a series of events.

Had Jason agreed to be the alligator he would be considered a friend by Joseph and Simon. They would later have told their families, "Jason is my friend." It is that easy when it works.

Friendship and fantasy form the natural path that leads children into a new world of other voices, other views, and other ways of expressing ideas and feelings they recognize as similar to their own. For adults, love and work may accomplish the same ends although, over the years,the overlay of unfulfilled expectations often puts obstacles in the way.To children,each new revelation of connectedness is a miracle.

If friendship and fantasy provide links to individual children, there is yet a third condition that completes the frame within which school makes sense: the need to become part of a larger group. It is the group that most influences the development of the storyteller.

Two friends alone will memorize each other's stories and learn a private language. But the storyteller is a culture builder, requiring the participation of an audience. Play is not enough; there must be a format that captures the essence of play while attaching to it a greater degree of objectivity. Storytelling and story acting can perform the task.

At this point Jason has not satisfied the first two needs, for he would seem to use fantasy to avoid friendship. Yet even a child who remains inside a helicopter can be reached once he realizes we offer him a legitimate audience for his fantasy.

Jason is not different from the rest of us. He too wants to tell his story. Why else does he roar his motor and openly complain about broken blades if not to capture our attention?

But attention, when begrudgingly given, does not satisfy for long. An idea must find the rhythm of a group to be fully communicated. The imagination is not a unilateral function; it thrives in the company of those who share its point of view and ask the right questions.

If Jason cannot yet be a friend to one other child, perhaps the less personal aspect of a larger audience will appeal to him. Playwriting need not involve reciprocity and can therefore side-step personal issues for a while. Story and stage provide a laboratory for every sort of child: those who are sociable but not articulate and those who speak better than they play; those who are trapped in a single theme and those who scurry quickly along the edges of too many. These are fertile grounds. Perhaps they will bear fruit for Jason.

Meanwhile, he provides me with new incentives to study the phenomenon. I want to know more about how, in the telling and performing of these stories, customs are invented that bind a group of children together,and how this effects everything else that happens in school.

Here is an intuitive and spontaneous set of responses from which teachers and children can create the rules and traditions that govern listening and responding. In the telling and performing of stories, all ideas must be heard, considered, compared, interpreted, and *acted upon*. The bridges built in play are lengthened,their partially exposed signposts organized and labeled in ways that commit the storyteller to travel in particular directions. The subject encompasses all of language and thought: *It is the academic inheritor of the creative wisdom of play.*

Always, we return to play, for storytelling and playwriting are also not enough. I must watch Jason at play even more closely than in the story room. How will the creative wisdom of *his* play express itself? Just as every storyteller begins with a unique message, the story player evolves an unparalleled relationship with those he eventually joins.

Even as I yearn for Jason to conform peacefully, I realize that conformity spoils a story. Had Jason's helicopter zoomed over and rescued the snakes, what would there be for me to watch and wonder about? Rescuing snakes is Joseph's story. What or whom will the helicopter boy decide to rescue? That is the intriguing question for me in this class.

"Jason, Jason, put your helicopter over here," Simon urges. "It's my squirrely runway. Pretend you don't see me and I'm in my squirrel hole and then you see me but first you don't."

Jason turns his back to the runway, but Simon is not deterred.

"Y'wanna land on the safe part?" There is still no answer. "Anyway," Simon shrugs, "I'm pretending it landed on my runway. I'm pretending it's O'Hare."

Though Jason ignores the children's play, he spends more time at the story table when they tell their stories.

"Would you like to tell a story?" I ask him one morning.

"I'm cutting a blade," he says.

"That could be a story. I could write down 'I'm cutting a blade.'"

"My blade is broken."

"I can put that in your story too. 'My blade is broken.'"

He doesn't answer, and I do not print the words. I can no more pretend Jason is dictating a story than I can pretend he is playing with Simon. Storytelling, in fact, is a more conscious invention than play. Simon can place his squirrel hole near Jason's airport and their several themes meet in midair, each child half listening to the other.

When Simon tells a story, however, he knows exactly what goes inside and what must be kept out. For one thing, his stories invariably begin with a little squirrel.

"Once there was a little squirrel. And there was a father. They finded a treasure map. Then they fighted a bad guy. That's Petey."

"I'll only be Mighty Mouse," Petey declares.

"There *is* Mighty Mouse in my story."

Simon alters any role to suit another child's fantasy. He is younger than Jason and, in his own way, more demanding—crying furiously when, in routine matters, his words or intentions are misunderstood. But once the wheels of fantasy begin to roll, he sees the point in contention more clearly and looks for a compromise or convincing argument.

"I mean Mighty Mouse pretends to be a bad guy but you're really not but I don't know it and then I know it."

Petey is satisfied. Pretending to be a bad guy when everyone knows you're good is the best of all possible worlds. He returns the favor by putting a little squirrel into his own Mighty Mouse story:

Mighty Mouse thinked that the house is on fire. It's
little squirrel's house. So he pushes the river over
the house to put the fire into water. It's all out.

The stage upon which we act out our stories is a taped square
in the center of the story room rug. It is sacrosanct when stories
are performed; the children learn to keep off stage unless they
are in the story. Jason refuses to abide by the rule and it upsets
everyone. His motor tunes up as each story begins, and within
a sentence or two he is flying around the stage. He does this
now as we act out Simon's story.

There is a question I have begun to ask. "Is there a helicopter
in this story?"

"No," Simon replies.

"Then you mustn't come on the stage, Jason."

Jason has heard this reasoning before. You may not enter a
story unless the author gives you a role to perform. Commentary is welcome at any time, but permission is required to insert
a new character into someone's story.

This is an easy concept to understand in the controlled setting
of a staged story, easier than in the doll corner, but in both
places the case for dramatic integrity is strong. It is an essential
aspect of the social contract and can be used as the basis for
solving most behavioral problems. Do your actions belong in
the scene you enter? If not, can you convince the players to
alter their script or, failing to do that, will you agree to a
different role? We call it socialization, which simply means—at
any age—that you play your part acceptably well in the given
script.

I resume Simon's story and again Jason forges loudly onto
the stage.

"Simon, is there a helicopter in your story? Do the squirrels
see a helicopter?" Simon can barely hear me over Jason's tu-
mult.

"No . . . uh, yeah, they do. They heered it flying over there.
Then it lands on *this* spot. Right here."

Jason winds down and stops on the designated place. "Br-ur-rumpt! I turned off the motor," he says. Jason has deliberately furthered another child's story. Why does he respond now and not earlier in the blocks when Simon asked him to land on the runway?

Perhaps many such experiences are required before it is safe to listen. Or does the safety come with being part of an audience, where a child can focus on an idea in a prescribed area and see his own behavior better through the eyes of all his peers. In any case, today Jason has listened.

The next day I tell Jason, "You turned off your motor when Simon told you to land. Now you know all about stories. Do you want to tell one?"

"Yes."

Is this more of my manipulation? I don't think so. It is simply a hunch, and hunches are also part of teaching. A child who listens and responds to another child's story may indeed be ready to tell his own to the group.

Jason begins immediately. "And a helicopter. A turbo prop. It's flying." How could his first story be anything else? Seldom would a child's initial attempt be so predictable. From this I gather that we are seeing the real Jason barricaded behind the walls of his airport. It is best not to tamper with such a genuine self-image. We must allow it to evolve as it will, in its own direction.

In the story room, Jason zooms around the rug as I read his story, continuing to fly several moments beyond the last words on the page. When he stops, I say, "I wonder if the helicopter sees another plane?"

"Someone," he answers.

"Which someone?"

"The squirrel someone."

Simon stands up. "He means me! I'm the plane, right?" Jason nods, and Simon imitates the helicopter roar we have come to know so well. Chins forward, arms in motion, the boys fly together in formation.

In this shaky process of school socialization there is no preordained script, but Jason himself has taken the first steps. He entered the classroom with a well-defined symbol and has kept it polished. Its roar drowns our words and sometimes angers or alarms those caught in its path. But Jason is visible. He projects a forceful image. He will not allow himself to be swallowed up by strangers in a strange place.

Those who never disrupt may be withholding too much. Until they tell us more of what is on their minds, they may not be able to listen to what *we* have to say. There is a tendency to look upon the noisy, repetitive fantasies of children as *noneducational*, but helicopters and kittens and superhero capes and Barbie dolls are storytelling aids and conversational tools. Without them, the range of what we listen to and talk about is arbitrarily circumscribed by the adult point of view.

If not for his squirrel hole, Simon might still be the tearful boy who entered school in September. His fantasy provided a safe retreat and still stimulates a whole network of plans and ideas.

Jason knows the importance of disguises. Before he used Simon's name, he called him "that squirrel someone." It is often easier to reach out in a fantasy role than in barefaced, confusing, adult-centered reality.

Perhaps, because Jason's own identity seems so unyielding, he has begun to ask the questions other children seldom do. "Why is he a lion?" he wants to find out about Alex who growls in stories every day.

Jason even puts the question into a story. "The airplane is spinning. It just the wheels go down and come up. There is a lion person." But when we act out his story, he says there is no lion person. "You made a mistake," Jason tells me.

"Why is she a mother?" he asks about Dana, whose mothers have many babies. In her most recent story she took eight babies to school.

"There's a baby in my story," Jason says. "A she-baby." I add the baby to his story but in the story room he is surprised. "Sarah's not in my story," he cries. It is his first mention of his baby sister.

The next day Katie puts a monster in her story and later, on the playground, Jason tugs on my arm. "There's a monster in my story," he whispers. But the monster does not appear. Jason is toying with the notion of a monster just as he wonders if he dares to mention a baby.

I wonder when she-babies and monsters will arrive in Jason's story or play. No two children develop the same relationship between image and story. Certainly every kind of learning differs from child to child, but nowhere are the behaviors more strikingly original than in storytelling. Even as the children borrow one another's ideas, they preserve a style and symbolism as unique as their fingerprints.

Katie's monster is on Jason's mind, but when he finally does allow a monster to enter his story, it will be quite different. Now, however, waiting to be picked up at noon, he practices her monster sentence over and over: "Then we saw a monster inside our room we saw a monster inside our room we saw a monster."

This is Katie's story:

> Once upon a time there was two little girls and a
> mommy and a daddy slept all together all in the
> same bed. And then they thinked of a monster with
> black ears and they put their capes on and creeped
> downstairs. And then we saw the monster inside
> our room.

"Creeped downstairs" comes from Ira. Every year certain phrases are planted and take root, the shoots continually coming up in stories and in play. Remember Joseph's alligator who creeped downstairs? The use of a communal symbol is as tangible a demonstration of socialization as the agreement to share blocks and dolls.

Ira's "creeped downstairs" story will be referred to throughout the year. "Once upon a time there was a boy who is five. And he was locked in his room," began Ira's story.

"Who locked him in?" Simon asked.

Without Simon's anxious question, Ira's story has less impact. The social and emotional effect of questions such as this one cannot be overestimated. Shortly, a major change in Jason's play will occur because of Ira's locked up boy and Simon's question. The very next sentence in the story, in fact, is in answer to Simon's question.

> He was locked in by his mother because he didn't want to take a nap. Then he creeped downstairs because he had a key. And there was Slime Man. He ran upstairs and locked all the doors. Happily ever after.

Simon is first to copy Ira's phrase. "The baby squirrel creeped downstairs and found a bad guy and bited him. Then the dad found his baby squirrel lying in the street." When you creep downstairs you find a bad guy; with Simon's story the connection is established.

"Creeped downstairs" is a literary and a cultural event. Whenever an idea is borrowed I call attention to the fact, but it is not within my power to manufacture a symbol. Each group chooses its own verbal banners.

"Simon's story has something in it that reminds me of Ira's."

"Creeped downstairs!" the children shout.

"I'm doing that," Petey says, and the next day Mighty Mouse "creeped downstairs and then he saw Slime Man and he flied out the window."

We read at least two books a day to the entire class and additional books to anyone who asks. With three teachers in the room, someone is usually available to read a book. Yet, the literary symbols and traditions taken up by a roomful of children are most likely to originate in their own stories.

Perhaps this is because adult authors cannot hear the hum

of a particular classroom or feel the instantaneous common experience, the suddenly revealed pleasure or fear. An outsider doesn't know Alex's lion growl or Jason's helicopter roar—or the feeling of creeping down the stairs after being locked in a room by one's own mother, an idea, in fact, that if found in an adult story would be far too frightening.

Nor would an outsider know that Lilly now ends many of her stories with a ritual of bedtime, meals, and teeth brushing.

> The little girl comes. The mother comes. The daddy.
> The brother. A dog. They go to sleep. They wake
> up. They have breakfast. Then they eat lunch. Then
> they eat dinner. They brush their teeth. They go to
> sleep. They wake up. They eat breakfast. The end.

No one is bored by the limitations of her plot. Indeed, nearly every hand is raised when she chooses her actors, and the symbols of security and dependability represented in her stories will be copied throughout the year.

Children are quick to interpret one another's intentions. We are never in error when we use the children's own language and imagery to help further their designs.

"It's silly," Jason says.

"What's silly?" I ask.

"This thing's eating draw."

"What does 'eating draw' mean, Jason?"

"It means eating draw."

Petey looks at Jason's paper. "He drawed on there and that's eating it," he explains. "Mine isn't because I don't use the white."

Now I see what Jason means. White on white is hard to see. The white paper eats the white crayon. The paper "eats draw."

"I'm having trouble drawing," Jason says.

"Don't use the white," I suggest. "Use another color. Then the paper won't eat draw."

"The blue won't eat it, Jason," Arlene says, giving him a blue paper. "Put the white on the blue."

Petey grabs the blue paper and flies it around Jason's head, letting it fall on the helicopter. "There, it landed."

"Your white is flying in the sky," Arlene says.

"First it hasta float like this whooosh," Jason says, making white circles on the blue paper. "Now it's going higher."

The children pick up an idea and play with it, improvising until it makes sense, which is to say, takes on the aspect of a story. It is almost impossible to explain something effectively to a child without using an image that has come from the child. If the paper "eats draw," then that is where to begin.

I am bombarded by such evidence of the distance between the children's world and mine. To me, Jason seems different from the others, but it is clear that I am the one who is different, not Jason. His thinking mirrors that of his classmates; their images creep into his play and his talk, and it is their solutions that cause him, from time to time, to stop whirling his blades in order to listen.

Cleanup time. Jason remains behind his wall of blocks. "I can't get out," he announces. "I'm all locked. I'm a bad guy."

"Who locked you in?" I ask.

"You did."

"I did?"

"Because I didn't take a nap." He uses Ira's idea instead of broken helicopter blades to explain his actions, but I am too bent on the cleanup schedule to celebrate.

"Jason, we need you to clean up. Right now."

"I'm locked."

"You need to come out, Jason."

My persistance makes him run for his old cover. "My blade is broken." He is on the verge of tears. "I have to fix them, don't you know? I'm locked, I told you!"

"Yeah, yeah, you could get out," Joseph grumbles. He can't bear for another child to continue playing after he has stopped. "Here, Jason. Here's the key. I found it. There, I unlocked you."

Jason steps out, hesitantly, and stares at Joseph who has already begun to dismantle the wall. The solution is logical, the sort used by child storytellers.

We cannot, of course, do without adult storytelling. The poetry and prose of the best children's books enter our minds when we are young and sing back to us all our lives.

Arlene quotes the mother duck in Robert McCloskey's *Make Way for Ducklings*. "Don't you worry. I know all about bringing up children," she'll say during some minor controversy in the doll corner. And she might add, "That looks like just the right place to hatch ducklings."

"And a quiet old lady who was whispering hush," Eli murmurs from inside a hunter's hut. "Psh-sh—a quiet old lady who was whispering hush psh-sh and a quiet old lady who was whispering hush." This line from Margaret Wise Brown's *Goodnight Moon* evokes the mood Eli needs as he sits alone taping his paper bow and arrow.

These verbatim bits of book dialogue bring a group closer together. The children understand that an appropriately used phrase from a favorite book has the power to release pleasurable memories of a special world held in common. Furthermore, the question of appropriateness is for the group to decide by its own usage.

Three lines from Marie Hall Ets's *In The Forest* are repeated by Lilly and Edward so often during transitional moments that the words have come to herald the beginning of a new activity: "Don't go away! I'll hunt for you another day." "We played Drop-the-Handkerchief once all around." "And our baby is no bother at all."

The last is said by a pair of kangaroos, and I find myself using it to mean, "Sorry to interrupt, but we'll have nearly as much fun in music as you're having in the blocks."

Simon breaks out of his squirrel hole at least once a week shouting, "Christopher Robin goes hoppity hoppity hoppity hop! Whenever I tell him politely to stop it he says he can't possibly stop." Simon's use of A. A. Milne's rhyme produces a smile from all who hear it and sometimes even the next line of verse or the recollection, "We did that on Alex's birthday!"

The culture of a particular classroom can be discovered only by listening to the children. Phrases from familiar books, of course, are immediately recognizable, but other connections may need to be acted out before they are understood.

"I'm a fluff," Arlene dictates.

"A piece of fluff?"

"No, a fluff," she answers, revealing nothing. But when her story is acted out, she says, "I need a daddy," and she blows herself off the daddy's coat.

The roles children give themselves cannot be accounted for with any certainty. Children, in fact, are surprised if someone thinks an explanation or justification is necessary. "Why are you always the baby?" makes no sense to a child. When Jason wondered about Alex being a lion, he was questioning not the idea that Alex is a lion but rather how Alex *knows* he's a lion.

Dana, in play, is the big sister or babysitter, but in her stories she's the baby. Edward is a superhero in the blocks but a bad guy who is killed in his stories. Simon, of course, is the baby squirrel whenever possible.

His mother complains, "What? Another squirrel story?" And Edward's mother worries, "Why must you be killed all the time?"

But the children applaud these decisions. For them, typecasting is the preferred model. When a storyteller needs a baby squirrel, he can depend on Simon. And Edward's daily death ritual supports the certain belief that the bad guy comes alive again as a good guy whenever he wishes. Jason's desire to be a helicopter is considered logical and beneficial. The children like to know who someone *is*.

The adult view seldom reflects the position taken by the children and once a childlike thought enters the scene, it captures the hearts and minds of the audience.

"Boys and girls, I'm sorry, but I must complain about cleanup again. People are going into the book room before they do a job."

"We should of made a trap door," Joseph says.

"All right. Let's just *pretend* there's a trap door," I suggest.

"No, it has to be a real one. I'll make you one." He takes a large piece of easel paper and begins to draw a maze of lines and arrows.

"Put the lock part over here," Alex directs.

"Let me do the stairs—or is it supposed to be a slide?"

"Yeah, Samantha, you do the slide and then the bad guy slides up here."

"I'll do the dungeon part," Edward offers. "And a key."

The children place their pictures on the book room floor and Joseph announces, "Whoever goes in there if they didn't clean up they fall down the trap door."

No one says, "This isn't a trap door." There is the spontaneous wish to believe the fantasy, to act in Joseph's trap door story. The children hurry through cleanup and report to Joseph, the chief of the cleanup project.

"I just slided up here, Joseph, and I wiped off a table, okay?"

"I put away a hundred blocks. Can I go?"

Joseph approves all claims. "I picked up a paper" receives the same smile as "I lifted sixteen big boards." We don't have a hundred blocks or sixteen boards, but it doesn't matter. The children have taken control of an adult problem and are acting out a solution. It may be a mock solution, a one-day wonder, but one day is a whole world and tomorrow there will be a new story.

Everyone assembles in the story room, ready to act out their stories. "Come with me, children," I say. "The cleanup job is not quite finished, although you did make a fine start."

The children follow me and look around curiously while I hand out specific jobs by name. There are no arguments; it is time for the teacher's reality to be acknowledged.

Back in the story room, Edward tells Joseph, "Remember the great cleanup job we did with the trap door?"

"Yeah, that was great. Hey, Jason, you missed a great job, you know." Jason attended to neither the pretend nor the real cleanup. "My blade is broken," he said. "I have to fix it now."

Whenever I think about the children's differences, my sense of the excitement of teaching mounts. Without the uniqueness of each child, teaching would be a dull, repetitive exercise for me. Every day, after the children leave, my assistants and I clean up quickly so we have time to compare revelations. Gail and Trish no longer wait for me to begin.

"Did you see Arlene counting in the marble game? She skips the blues because 'they like to be numbered by theirself.'"

"How about Jason with the colors? I'm certain he knows all the colors but when I asked why he paints every helicopter purple, he told me they were green and yellow."

"But, really, Joseph is just as perplexing," I chime in. "You know the game I invented, with the arrows? When I set it up on the table, Joseph rushed over and said, 'I know that already. You don't have to show me how.' So of course he missed the whole point until after he watched Arlene and Samantha play the game twice."

"Here's something you didn't see. After snack, Jason took the game into his airport and used the arrows for blades."

"Hmm. Interesting. Because, you know, he wouldn't let me show him the game at all."

We speak of surprises, seldom of certainties. We want to talk about what we don't understand and what has not worked out according to expectations. My assistants are relative newcomers to teaching, and they tell me this is a useful approach to the subject: What did we find out today that we didn't know yesterday and for which we have no answer?

Gail and Trish fill their pockets with scraps of paper on which they note the "good" incidents, the kind that point to misunderstandings and how these come about.

"Remember Edward's story where a tall person rocked and rocked and you thought he meant in a rocking chair?" Gail asks me.

"Didn't he?"

"No, he meant getting under rocks and breaking out of a trap."

"How did you find out?"

"I heard him in the blocks. He told Eli—wait, let me find it— here, he said, 'Pretend you're rocking then you rock under the rocks. Then you rock and rock the rocks to pieces and you break out of the trap.'"

Trish nods. "Gail's right. See, Vivian, your comment threw him off the track. It made him doubt his own common sense. He knew he didn't mean rocking chair but you were so certain rocking had to do with a chair that he forgot why he was hammering when he acted out those words."

"What exactly did I say?"

"Something like, 'Is that a different kind of rocking chair?'"

At home, I replay the tape and transcribe my exact question. "Is there a rocking chair on the mountain?" was what I asked Edward. This was when he stopped hammering and looked confused. Then he covered up his confusion by falling down.

The next day, I tell Edward, "Mrs. Taylor told me I made a mistake in your story, and when I listened to my tape, I saw that she was right. I made a big mistake."

"What was it?"

"Well, you said rocked and rocked and I thought you meant a rocking chair."

He smiles. "Why did you?"

"Probably I didn't listen and watch carefully enough. Because you *were* hammering."

"I was breaking rocks. We was in a trap."

"Now I do understand, Edward. 'Rocking' comes from rocks. Breaking rocks."

This is not too much time to give to words and their meanings. The children learn that figuring out what we do and say and read and play are equally important. Everything is supposed to make sense; if it doesn't, ask questions, go over it again, find out why the picture is blurred. The range of possibilities for misunderstandings is quite astonishing. And is this not a lucky circumstance? It means we ought never to run out of great curriculum materials, free for the asking. We only need to listen for our own errors and there is enough text to fill the school year.

After school. "I told Edward about my mistake with the rocking chair."

"What did he say?" Trish asks.

"He smiled. He knew I'd made an error. I guess he just didn't know how to correct me right then and there. So he fell down and acted silly . . . By the way, Gail, do you keep a record of all the stories?"

"Only the stuff I want to talk about," she replies.

"For me it works the other way," I say. "If I don't write it down, I can't figure out what it means. Talk is not enough."

"Do you have a helicopter in your story?" It is Jason speaking. He has taken me by surprise. The question is directed to Arlene who has just begun her story about a little girl, a mother, and a crocodile.

"Is there a helicopter in there?" Jason asks again. He sits across the table from us adding helicopter pictures to a large pile in front of him. As he completes each one he twirls it over his head and lets it fall on the stack of papers. Now he holds one poised over his head and asks, for the third time, "Is there a helicopter in your story?"

"Is it too noisy?" Arlene responds, finally. She seems as startled as I am. Jason has borrowed the question I ask on his behalf nearly every day, but he is anticipating the conflict in a completely original way. He comes around the table and drops the picture on Arlene's story. "It's already going to land. I turned off the motor."

On his own, Jason has given his symbol to another child to be used according to her judgment. In addition, he has invented a new idea. No one in this class has ever drawn a character for someone else's story. The idea could catch on or be a one-time-only literary device. The group will judge its usefulness.

Arlene does decide to use the picture in her story, and she allows Jason to hold it as it lands "outside the window."

"The helicopter creeped down the stairs," Jason says. "Then it landed."

It is Jason's imagination that begins to creep downstairs to where the children are, stepping from phrase to phrase, from story to story, onto a runway that is built by the entire class.

However, a boy who would be a helicopter cannot be expected to spin his blades in the same way as, let's say, someone who invents trapdoors and magic keys. Traps and keys capture and release people; rotating blades usually keep people away. Furthermore, it is easier to give away a picture and borrow a phrase than to commit yourself in friendship.

The next day, Jason pulls back. He may feel he is moving out too fast, losing ground without being certain enough of the territory.

"I want to I always have to be a helicopter do you always tell me not to!" he complains angrily to me.

"I didn't tell you not to be a helicopter, Jason. But Simon asked you to come into his squirrely hole and I thought you didn't hear him since you didn't answer."

"Because that squirrely guy is outside the window!" Jason shouts.

It takes Simon a moment to grasp Jason's meaning. "I'm not outside! Don't say that!" Now Simon is angry, and Jason seems surprised that his fanciful statement has received such an intense response.

"That squirrel someone is outside," Jason repeats, red-faced, forcing a smile.

"I hate you, Jason! You're never my friend!" Simon is crying and Jason turns away quickly. "My blade is broken."

"I'm sorry Jason made you cry, Simon," I say, bringing him

tissues. "Maybe he didn't know you would mind so much if he said that."

"Yeah, he did know I mind so much. He's not coming to my birthday!" Simon feels relieved, proclaiming the ultimate threat, but Jason has not yet discovered its meaning.

Or perhaps he has. His story of the day reflects a different mood, confusion about his own purposes.

> There's a no-helicopter in my story. A not-helicopter.
> It's a not-airplane. My helicopter is in it. The heli-
> copter goes up to the sky. Then crash! This helicop-
> ter. Crash! Then I fix it. A not-airplane story.

Jason will not allow his helicopter to become too acculturated. In the story room later, when I make the mistake of complimenting him on his cooperative behavior, he reminds me sharply that I am not to take him for granted.

I have begun reading Alex's story. "It's about a lion and a monkey and two bad guys . . ."

"Woo-ooo-woo-ooo!"

"Stop it, Jason. There's no helicopter in here." I begin again. "And the lion went . . ."

"Br-r-r-eeee-ah!"

"Alex, is there a helicopter in your story?"

"No."

"Woo-ooo-ooo!"

"Jason, you must stop now."

Jason runs to the window. "Yeah, I hear it. It's in the story. A helicopter, a helicopter!"

"No! Don't say that in my story."

"Ooo-ooo! Look!"

"No, it's *my* story, Jason!"

"There's starting the blades!"

Alex runs over to Jason and gives him a light push. "Wait, Alex," I say. "Let's just do the story. Jason is so excited right now it's hard for him to stop. Come on. He'll stop when he's ready. I'll read very loudly, okay?"

We manage to get through story time. The children are not

bothered by Jason's outbursts as much as I am. In fact, after Alex's initial anger, there seems to be an equal interest in the printed stories and Jason's plans to disrupt them.

The children have many more safe and ingenious ways to deal with frustrations than I have. At the end of the morning, when I am washing paint jars and Trish and Gail are with the rest of the class on the playground, Alex and Arlene blast Jason into a million pieces.

They are alone at the sand table, plotting his demise. I hear the first part of the fantasy as I gather up the dirty jars, but my tape recorder saves the surprise ending for me: Jason is to reenter the world as their baby.

Arlene: In five minutes this tissue turns to magic. I wetted it. Is five minutes over yet?

Alex: The kind me and Simon made? First we buried something in the sand and then it's all buried and that magic is helping us make it magical.

Arlene: To blast people?

Alex: To blast Jason. To the sky. Because he keeps fighting us, even just me in the story room.

Arlene: Tissue in the sand. He'll be blasted?

Alex: To a million pieces.

Arlene: The whole world forever.

Alex: Let's lift up the whole sandbox. Help me. Superman can carry the whole school up and we'll all fall in the river.

Arlene: But not us, right? But everyone else. But not our mom and dad. Only Jason?

Alex: And Joseph. And Petey. Not Simon. Blast them to pieces in the helicopter. Put them here. This is the helicopter.

Arlene: They'll blast to french fries and we'll eat them up. Not Samantha and Katie.

Alex: I can't wait to do this. First we explode Jason.

Arlene: Then we fix him up, right? Then he's our baby. Our new baby.

Alex: Yeah, and I'm the superdad and you're the su-
            permom.

The power of fantasy play to restore balance and ballast can
never be overestimated. This is the point I make the next day
when I read the transcript of the sand table play to Trish and
Gail.

"Without the tape recorder, you wouldn't have known the
lovely ending to the story," Trish comments.

"I'll bet there are loads of these upbeat endings that we don't
get the chance to hear," I say. "It ought to make us very
cautious about the judgments we announce."

"Speaking of judgments, how come you let Jason interrupt
all the stories yesterday?"

"I didn't *let* him. I simply couldn't prevent him from doing
it. The children saw that. They know I'm not willing to get
nasty just to prove my power."

"But what if other children start doing the same sort of
thing?" Gail asks. "I worry about that."

"They don't. The one child who *has* to disrupt, does it. The
rest watch. And especially, they watch the teacher to see if that
unsettled child is safe from harm. That's all they want to
know."

Trish and Gail look doubtful. "Okay. You two will figure
these things out for yourselves when you have your own classrooms. But for me, Jason's behavior in the story room was
annoying but in no way harmful. Had I moved in with force—
separating him from the group, punishing him in some way—
that would be harmful to the group. For then I would have
admitted to a lack of faith in the power of reason and good will
to solve our problems, not necessarily on the spot, but eventually."

"Sometimes it's not the kind of problem that can be solved
by good will," Trish says.

"Such as?"

"Well, wouldn't some people call what Jason does 'perseveration'?"

"I can't tell you what someone who uses that label would say about Jason," I reply. "By the way, notice how close it is to 'persevere,' yet one word suggests pathology and the other a sense of strength and self-direction."

Gail is already leafing through the dictionary. "Here," she says."'Perseveration: continuation of something to an exceptional degree or beyond a desired point.' Okay, next. 'Persevere: to persist in a state, enterprise, or undertaking in spite of counter influences, opposition, or discouragement.'"

Trish looks worried. "Then is it only a matter of semantics? All these terms I'm learning, are they just arbitrary—uh, made-up . . .? I mean, don't these problems slow a child down?"

"Look, Trish, I'll admit I've little faith in your lists of so-called learning disabilities. But, in any case, none of these labels apply in a classroom that sees children as storytellers. These labels don't describe the imagination. A storyteller is always in the strongest position; to be known by his or her stories puts the child in the most favorable light."

Trish jumps up. "Of course! I really do see what you mean. How can a storyteller be fast or slow?"

Gail laughs. "And these children are not a stable of race horses trained by us to go faster and slower."

"Exactly," I add. "The teacher can forget the words *fast* and *slow*."

"Good! That's one more thing I don't need to worry about," Trish says, giving me a big smile.

The sand table fantasy may have been satisfying, but evidently Alex needs a more permanent position paper on Jason. The following morning he tells this story:

> Once some lions had a baby lion. And then at night-
> time the baby cried. Something was bothering the
> baby when he slept at night. And then he knew it
> was outside that you could hear it. It was a helicop-

ter that was outside and the baby lion couldn't sleep. Now they had a new rule: No helicopter can come at night. The end.

In the story room, I say, "Jason, there's something in Alex's story I must show you. I know you can't read, but I'll point to the words and tell you what they say."

Jason comes quickly; this is a new behavior from the teacher. "Look, here, where my finger is. This says, 'They had a new rule: No helicopters come in the night.'"

"Show me again," Jason says.

"I wanna see it," several children shout, and I ask Alex to take his paper around and show it to everyone. He holds the story close to each child's face and pretends to read the message. "No helicopter ever can come in the night. The end."

I retrieve Alex's story and place it in the pile of stories on my lap. "We'll do Jason's story first," I say, and he tumbles into the center of the rug.

"Mine's going to crash so the baby doesn't wake up," he tells me. Then he repeats his entire story before I can read it. "Mine has some propellers are Y's and some are X's." He shows us the letter shapes with his fingers and arms, racing around at his fastest speed and highest decibel. "Crash!" he shouts, falling flat on the rug. He returns to his seat and does not interrupt the stories that follow, though several times he comes to see Alex's rule.

The next morning, Jason puts his finger on the bottom of the page and says, "My rule is here."

"What is the rule?"

"A helicopter."

"A rule about a helicopter?"

"The rule is helicopter."

I print his word an inch from the bottom in the right-hand corner. "Put my nuther rule here." He points to the middle of the page.

"What rule goes here?"

"Helicopter."

"Do you want to draw a picture of a helicopter instead of me writing it?"

"A picture can't be a rule. And one goes here and one goes here and here." Before we are done, Jason has located six more "rules." Then he begins his helicopter rumble, touching each word as he starts the motors.

"What's Jason doing?" Joseph asks, giving Jason's helicopter a slight push along the table. "Why does his story look like that, teacher?"

Before I can answer, Jason whines and pulls at Joseph's hand. "Don't touch my helicopter!"

"Mmmm," Joseph hums softly. "Mmmm just looking at it mmm." Slowly he begins to turn the blades. I watch in trepidation; no one is allowed to handle the helicopter.

"Mmmm pshshsh here you go mmm."

"It's broken. I have to fix it," Jason cries, pushing Joseph away.

"Can you show it to me?" Joseph asks softly. "Does it go mmmm?"

Jason relaxes. "It can't go now. I didn't put in the fuel."

"Pshsh mmm, here's the fuel, nice little helicopter," Joseph continues, aiming an imaginary nozzle and keeping his hand on the plane. "Where's the wheels?"

"Under here," Jason says, looking as if he might be stifling a scream as Joseph continues to move the helicopter.

"Mmm hey Jason y'wanna come to my house mmm along you go mmm pshpshpsh there you go mmm here you are mmm slowing down down mmm." It is a helicopter lullaby. Everyone at the table watches quietly; the moment is intimate, soothing and calming.

"Hey, Joseph! Come over here!" Alex shouts. "Look what I brang!"

"I gotta go, Jason. Here's your helicopter."

Jason stares at Joseph as he disappears into a snake hideout. Then Jason turns back to his story paper filled with rules. "And the end. Here. Where it lands."

"I think I know what your story is, Jason. You'll land on each place where it says helicopter?"

"That's the rule," he states.

"The rule is, wherever it says helicopter you have to land. Will you land on the paper or on the rug?"

"On the rule." He grabs his helicopter story and dives into his airport. "Don't touch my helicopter, Joseph," he says. "Are you going to?"

"I won't."

Jason and his helicopter are an intriguing pair. Although he knows he is Jason, separate from a helicopter, in anxious moments, surrounded by lots of people, the boundaries blur. The distinction is no problem when he can act out his own story and be a helicopter, but the constantly changing stories of his classmates on the stage worry him as they seldom do in the block area, where a tangible structure shields him from other fantasies.

The difference, then, between the story room and the block area would seem to be a matter of territoriality. Once his story has been acted out, he can no longer see, touch, or defend a private landing place. This may be why he decides to land his helicopter on the paper and carry the story paper with him.

One line of guessing I don't bother with is what the helicopter ultimately represents to Jason; my task is to figure out how his symbol can carry him to safety in our classroom.

Meanwhile, we talk about the problem of the moment, in hopes of reaching a solution for the day. I tell what I think, the children tell what they think, and our mutual interest in what Jason thinks is a good substitute for settling the issue.

We can never fully discover the essential issues for each child or set up the perfectly safe environment. What we do is continually demonstrate the process of searching for solutions. This is the point at which studying becomes teaching.

"Jason, sometimes you still run into the stage even if it's not your turn."

"My blades are spinning."

"But it seems as if your blades spin more in the story room than in the blocks."

"Because he makes a airport there to land," Samantha points out.

"Could that be the reason?" I wonder.

"Yeah, it really is the reason," Joseph states with assurance. "Aren't you sad because you don't have a airport in here to land? To *stay* landed?"

Jason is surprised by the question, but Joseph interprets his silence as agreement. "See, I told you. He's sad because there's no airport. His helicopter needs one."

"Is Joseph right? Jason, if you had an airport in here, would your helicopter stay landed? The children think it will."

"Yes," he answers, doubtfully, not following the consequences of the discussion.

"The problem is," I remind everyone, "this is a small room. We already have a rule about not bringing blocks in here."

"Let him make a small airport," Arlene says. "Just two blocks."

"I want to." Jason's face is shining with expectation. "Two blocks."

"Let him do it!"

"Do it, do it, Jason!" The children jump about in a wild display of happiness. There are few classroom experiences as exhilarating as one in which we help a classmate escape from a trapdoor.

Jason brings two large blocks to the story room every day now and builds a "heliport." He changed the name at Edward's bidding.

"Call it a heliport, Jason."

"A airport."

"No, it isn't, Jason. Say heliport if you want to be the right way."

"Heliport."

"O-*kay*. Now you got it!" Edward gives Jason a heavy-handed pat on the back.

Jason does not like to be touched by the children, but he takes the friendly smack in stride, along with the new label. Actually, Jason has used "heliport" before, but his acceptance of the term at this point is clearly intended to please Edward.

The fact is Jason is listening more carefully to the words children use as they play. They are all words he knows, but he hears them now in a new social context and they have a deeper meaning. In so doing, he enlarges his repertoire of responses each day, beyond his fixed helicopter rituals.

"Call it tornado," Alex tells Simon. "I'm Superman and you're Superman Tornado."

"No, I'm a squirrel that turned into Superman Tornado."

The boys have begun to build less than three feet from Jason's heliport. "Don't touch my heliport," Jason has said three times. "Don't tornado this place," he adds.

"This is the ice castle. It don't touch nothing or it could kill you. You know what Simon? Superman doesn't need a door. He flies up, right?"

"Watch out, water with sharks!"

"The sharks don't eat Superman."

Samantha runs up. "Look, you guys. I have a bunny that I can turn into anything I like."

"We're playing Superman."

"So what? I'm She-Ra. Hey, Jason, I need that block for my castle."

"I'm using it!" he screams. "It's my tornado block."

"Just give me one and I'll be your friend, okay?"

"Okay," Jason replies.

"Thanks, Mr. Tornado block." Samantha does nothing more to prove she's a friend, but Jason watches her curiously. This may be the first time in class someone has uttered those magic words to him. "I'll be your friend."

"Don't put Crystal Castle near here, Samantha," Alex says. "We're playing Darkside. He'll kill you." He aims a thumb and forefinger at Mirka who has just joined Samantha in Crystal Castle with a supply of pillows and blankets.

"Wait a minute! She's Wonderwoman!" Samantha yells. "You don't bang at Wonderwoman."

"So what! You're under arrest. Let's get out of here, men. Trouble in West End!" The boys scramble out of the Ice Castle and run toward the cubby room.

"No running," I call out between words on the story paper, and the boys slow down to a fast walk until out of sight.

Jason sits down at the story table and tells me, "You don't bang at Wonderwoman."

"Because she's good?"

"I don't know."

"Let's ask Samantha. Samantha, why do people not bang at Wonderwoman?"

"Because she's magic. No one can kill her."

"Jason," I ask. "Do you know anything that's magic?"

"No." He twirls his blades. "The tornado is magic."

"The one Joseph was playing?"

"My tornado block. I made a tornado block. A *tornado* block. It's still in my airport. Tornado airport."

I write down "tornado" on the list of words and phrases that constitute Jason's spontaneous progress report.

"I need something to cut this," Jason says.

"Here's a scissors. What are you cutting?"

"Something that kills me."

"What do you call it?"

"Something that kills me." He cuts a long strip. "This is what I'm cutting."

"It's just a helicopter blade, Jason," Katie says, scribbling on her wolf picture to make the wolf "smoked out and squished up." She has just told another of her three pigs stories in which the wolf blows down the houses and the mother pig rebuilds them.

"It's something that kills me," Jason repeats.

"Are you thinking about Joseph banging at people?"

"I'm thinking about a tunnel. A big airplane is parked on the tunnel." He brings a large, curved, wooden shape and stands it on the story paper. "This is my story."

"I can't write the words if the tunnel is on the paper. Can you move it?"

"It can't move."

"Hold it *over* the paper until I finish. Then put it down again."

He lifts the tunnel barely high enough for me to move the pen along. "A big airplane it's such a big one you haven't believe it." Now he takes my pen and draws a line across the paper. "Jet stream. Oh, this thing that kills me turned into a blade. Get in there blade. Under the tunnel."

Jason is playing inside his story. My intention, of course, is that every story be played in, but Jason plays in his *on* the paper. He'll use the story room to act a scene he can't visualize linearly.

"I'm busy falling. Pk-k-k. Have me someone doing that."

"You want someone falling down going pk-k-k?"

"He wants a bad guy," Joseph explains. "Like in my story falling down dead."

"Is that so, Jason?" He nods and falls again. "Pk-k-k."

"Is it you? Are you the bad guy?"

Jason continues to fall, each time taking a harder bump. "Stop, Jason. Your story is over. Don't bump your head like that."

"I always do that," he says.

"It's not a good idea. You're getting a mark on your forehead." I take his hand and walk him to his seat. "It's Katie's turn, Jason. Come on, sit in the heliport."

The image of a jail door banging shut flashes before me. Did I encourage the story room heliport in order to contain Jason? If so, the solution will be short-lived. Perhaps even now he sees himself as a bad guy because he's surrounded by walls.

Katie bounds onto the stage. "No helicopters! No falling! No nothing, Jason, if I don't say it!"

He falls down one last time, knocking over his heliport wall, but he stands it up again quickly and says to himself, "Something that would kill me."

Katie hops around waving her arms at Jason. His behavior has excited her. I read through the story quickly: ". . . and the wolf blows the houses down."

"Wait, he blows them down again!" she shrieks. "Joseph has to keep blowing it down and I keep falling and then I put it back and then you blow it down and . . ." She is giddy with inspiration. Joseph joins her in tumbling around the room. "Make the chimney! Get the pot!"

Does Jason realize that his behavior has triggered this scene? His impulsive falling down and jumping up has led directly to Katie's image of a wolf repeatedly blowing down the pigs' house while their mother puts the house back together. Katie, the controlled and reasonable mother, sees enough logic in Jason's actions to apply them to her own.

Once again it is the children who explain Jason to me. They find his eccentricities understandable and not at all strange. What is wrong with twirling and fixing your blades or falling down if this is part of your act? You are supposed to be as ostentatiously dramatic as you can be at all times. So say the children by their own actions.

Furthermore, these same children, who argue so ferociously over the equal distribution of blocks and cookies and pink paint, defend a classmate's right to display unusual characteristics and make inconvenient demands. The children's concept of fairness is not limited by conformity; they want the equal opportunity to demand special treatment. It is unfair for Jason to disrupt a story, but he has the right to be the only one who builds a story room heliport.

The adult objection: What if everyone decides to become a helicopter and build a heliport? But the children know this never happens. The classroom doesn't need two helicopters. True, a rush of helicopters could occur, but they would quickly fade, leaving the one true pretender.

"Why do you always bring a helicopter?" the children asked Jason in the beginning.

"The blade is broken. I have to fix it." This was considered a sensible answer by all but me. I see my role more clearly now: to discover which of Jason's responses are deemed sensible by the children while observing which of our responses seem logical to Jason.

"Someone's hiding in my airport," Jason says, pointing to Simon.

"No! I'm not in there."

"Simon's in my airport."

"You're lying, you doody-head!"

"Simon's in my airport."

"Don't say my name! Tell him not to, teacher."

"Jason, Simon doesn't want you to pretend he's in your airport. Do you want him to come in? Really come in?"

"No."

Jason is not being sensible and the children refuse to accommodate him. No one offers to come into his house or to allow him to pretend they are hiding in there. Is Jason trying to invite Simon in or is he teasing?

"Jason, can I help you find someone to play inside your airport? Teachers do that, you know. Once I helped Simon find a mother squirrel, remember, Simon?"

"I don't want a mother squirrel," Jason says.

"Who do you want?"

"Someone hiding in my airport."

"Okay. Listen, everyone. Jason needs someone to hide in his airport. Who will do that?"

"Only if I can be the mother," Samantha says.

"It's a helicopter house."

"I'll be the mother and you're the baby."

"No."

"I'm She-Ra and you're the helicopter."

"Yes."

Samantha enters gingerly and sits down next to Jason, who says, "My blades are broken. I'm fixing them."

"We have to make beds. I'll get the pillows. Save my place."

Jason covers Samantha's place with one hand and blows on the helicopter blades. "Turn around, turn around, oooo not such a good spinning. Kick the house down, kick the house down."

Samantha returns with the bedding. "Lie down, little heli-copter," she says, making Jason into a baby as delicately as she can.

"Kick the house down."

"Sh-sh-sh little helicopter." If Samantha has tricked Jason into being a baby it is no less than Jason attempted to do with Simon, but she uses finesse. There is much to learn about play when you don't come to it easily.

Jason does not understand the play of other children, but they seem to know what he is playing. Luckily, he repeats his misconceptions and continues to act them out so that we can see them and react to them.

> There's a helicopter. They did not make such a good
> spinning. Then some things were blowing. It puffed
> the flying thing to a good place. The end.

"Was something wrong with the helicopter? Why didn't it make such a good spinning, Jason?"

"Because . . . there's a lot of too many people in the air."

"Oh, it was too crowded. By the way, Jason, did the blocks seem too crowded to you before?"

"No."

"I wondered, because you were saying 'Kick the house down.'"

"Because the helicopter didn't spin."

"Were you worried because Samantha was the mother?"

"Then the helicopter couldn't make a good spinning."

"Anyway, I'm glad you let Samantha in."

"Why are you?"

"Because it made her happy. That's why."

Soon I will have even more reason to feel glad, for, with this simple mother-baby episode, Samantha launches a whole-hearted pursuit of Jason that more than any other event in the school year brings him out of the helicopter house and into the social life of the classroom. Samantha is determined to make Jason into her baby and, despite his protestations and rituals, in the end she succeeds. Which is not to say she has the last word in his affairs; a boy who would be a helicopter enters society in full control of his vehicle.

Eli has a new way of choosing actors. "Someone with blue pants," he says, looking at Edward. "Someone with red lines," and Petey comes forward in his striped shirt.

The children examine their clothing, eager to be called. They love the rules they invent themselves. Once, when I changed the words of a folk song so that, with each new verse, children with specified colors were to skip around the room, there was a sense of discontent. My rule seemed too exclusive. "Don't worry. I'll call all the colors," I sang out, but my scheme did not bring the pleasure I'd anticipated.

Eli's color code is greeted with much interest and no anxiety. When it is Vinnie's turn, she uses shoes as a category. "Who is ever wearing Minnie Mouse shoes is the sister." Everyone looks at Katie whose Minnie Mouse sneakers are famous. She skips around the room, an actor with a mission.

I am impressed by the children's spontaneous lesson in classification and would like to expand it, but the idea is never repeated. It is a one-day novelty, having little to do with storytelling and acting. The children are less likely than I am to introduce non sequiturs. The rituals that last throughout the year all involve some aspect of the story itself.

Samantha, for example, now says "Once upon a time" several times when she begins a story. There was immediate approval for her idea, and the number of "Once upon a times" has grown. Alex wanted nine; I showed him that it took up most of the page. In fact, since storytellers are generally limited to one page, there was room for only one additional sentence: "There was a lion and he saw a bad guy."

"What shall we do?" I ask the group. "Some people keep saying 'Once upon a time' and there is hardly any space for a story."

"Make a rule to say it once," suggests Arlene, who is often first to suggest limits for others, all the while insisting on full freedom of action for herself.

"No, it's my idea," Samantha argues.

"Write it very tiny," Dana says.

"No, say it fast," Joseph declares, rattling off "onceponti-meoncepontimeoncepontime" breathlessly.

"Those are both good ideas. How about if I write tiny words for people who want me to—or, here's something I could do. We can say it fast, but I'll write 'Once upon a time' only once, with a number after it to tell us how many times to say it."

Joseph nods without understanding. The concept is too complex and needs help from me. This is one of those occasions when I must offer an answer whether or not the children fully comprehend.

I tack a blank page to the board and write down "Once upon a time." Then I turn to Samantha, since it *is* her idea. "Do you want it three times?"

"No, five."

"All right. Watch me. I put a 5 after 'Once upon a time.' Now, we'll *say* it five times, but I won't write it down five times. See how much space is left?"

The children stare at my paper. My explanation is not convincing. "Here, let me show you with Alex's paper. Look. Alex told me to write it nine times. Let's count the lines." We count the nine introductions to Alex's story.

"All right. Now, I'll cross out all of these except the first. Instead, I'll write 9. That will mean we have to say it nine times."

"Why did you make a X?" Alex asks, worried.

"I was trying to show that the 9 takes the place of all those 'Once upon a times.' We can say them but I won't copy them all down."

"And then you make a X?"

"Well, I won't have to. Here, let me show what it will look like." I take a fresh piece of paper and begin again. Oddly enough, the children are not restless. Without understanding what I am doing, they nonetheless seem fascinated by my performance.

"Now, pretend Alex is just beginning to tell me his story. Go on, Alex, start the lion story again."

"Once upon a time . . ." he begins, self-consciously.

"How many do you want?"

"Twelve."

"Okay. This says twelve. I wrote 'Once upon a time' just *once,* but I put 12 next to it. You've got the whole page left for your story, Alex."

"There was a lion," he continues, while I print his words for everyone to see. As the story itself takes over, he no longer feels awkward.

> And he saw a bad guy but first he didn't see him
> because the bad guy was in a tree but he heard
> something strange. Then he saw the bad guy so he
> asked him "Why are you in a tree?" "Because some-
> one said I was bad." So the lion told him he wasn't
> bad. So he came down. The end.

We are at the bottom of the page. "Now, look everyone. On this page there was no room for such a long story. Because all these sentences say 'Once upon a time.'"

"And the X," Alex reminds me. The X bothers him. I should have used lines through each "Once upon a time."

"Yes, and the X too. But now let's say 'Once upon a time' nine times. Count on our fingers." At the end of the count, I read Alex's story triumphantly. I have proven my point.

But Alex adds, "Because a tree is long. You have to have a lot of room." He jumps up and reaches his finger to the 9. "That's where the bad guy is sitting." Then his finger trails down to the bottom of the page. "This is the grass where he comes down." To a non-reader, the letters look like grass blowing in the wind and the 9 is a bad guy's seat.

The children understand Alex completely. We act out his story as if nothing unusual has happened. Yet I feel in the presence of a great universal truth: There are an infinite number of approaches to every concept. One can only wonder at the risks involved in grabbing a single way of looking at a topic and presenting it as a "lesson."

Jason tells me "nine" the next day when it is his turn on the list.

"Nine what?"

"Once."

"Nine onces?"

He pushes my pen. "Here . . . here . . . here . . . here . . . is that nine?" At his direction I print "once" in nine places. This is Jason's way of thinking about yesterday's discussion. Is it strange simply because no one else does it this way?

"You're remembering Alex's nine 'Once upon a times.'"

"I'm remembering once," he says, more accurately.

The children and I seem to spend a lot of time *pretending* Jason is part of our activities. Though our means are quite different, I wonder if our purposes might be the same: to make Jason fulfill our expectations.

My approach is to act as if Jason is purposefully making a contribution to the group even when it is clear this is not his intention. In music, for example, we are singing "Pawpaw Patch," a great favorite. Each child, in turn, sits inside a large crate pretending to be lost, while another child skips around trying to "find" the lost person. We sing "Where oh where is our friend Lilly . . ." until the partner discovers her and the two skip along together back to their seats.

Jason refuses his turn. "My blade is broken," he tells me. However, when I suggest that he put his helicopter in the crate and pretend to find it, he agrees to the plan. The children think it is a wonderful idea and decide to follow suit. Arlene hides her doll inside the crate, Joseph uses his snake as a partner, and the game continues "in Jason's way."

The problem is: *I'm* the one who calls it "Jason's way." I continue to remind everyone that this is his idea, but Jason pays little attention once his turn is over. After a while, the children switch back to people partners and "Jason's way" is forgotten.

That Jason has been singled out for special attention is good, but to give him credit for the idea just because he agreed to go along with it briefly is confusing—and dishonest as well. The children know which ideas are theirs and which are mine. I must be careful, in my desire that Jason become a full participant, not to obscure the truth.

I didn't pretend that Joseph had the idea for substituting numerical symbols for the "Once upon a time" column. Having faith in Joseph, I took his exact words—"say it fast"—and added my own idea to help the plan work. The children perceived the distinction between Joseph's role and mine.

My idea was not even clear to them until Alex envisioned the long tree with a robber sitting inside the 9. If nothing else does it, this experience ought to teach me never to pretend an idea of mine has come from a child.

As for Jason and the "Pawpaw Patch," I should have said, "Jason doesn't want a partner so I suggested he might want to use his helicopter."

The children are far more direct in their strategies, and it is easier for Jason to examine and think about what they say and do. In the following example from the doll corner, Jason again refuses to participate, as he did in the music room, but the children will not allow him to escape from accepting a token of responsibility to the group for making a fantasy work.

Jason is seated alone at the doll corner table, rolling out playdough into snake-like shapes, when Simon, Edward, and Lilly enter.

"Oh good," Edward says. "There's a snake hunter. Hey, me too, Jason. You catched the animals to cook. I shotted a tiger."

Jason moves his helicopter closer to his snake collection and covers them with his hands as the children continue to organize the scene.

"Me and Lilly are the cookers," Simon says. "I mean I'm the hunter waitress."

"But who's Jason?" Lilly wants to know.

Jason will not respond, and it is seen as a problem. Unlike the music room, where the children expect the teacher to say, "Okay, you can just watch," or the block area, where a child can build a self-contained unit, the doll corner houses one drama at a time. An unresponsive occupant may cause the same concern as would a stranger seated at our kitchen table at home. Is this fair? The children think so and, luckily for Jason, there is no adult present to apply a different sort of logic.

"Jason, yes or no, are you a hunter?" Edward persists.

Simon clarifies the rules. "No helicopters, Jason. You can be a hunter or a waitress."

"Or a dad?" Lilly says hopefully.

"No, Lilly. I'm the dad hunter. Or he could be a robber. Robbers! Robbers! Robbers in the restaurant! Call the police!" Edward, it would seem, has now decided Jason must go, or the plot will never be advanced. "No helicopters in the restaurant. This is only for hunters and waitresses and a dad and a mom. Okay, so?"

Jason suddenly rises, looks about him with a frown, and removes all doubt. "I'm a helicopter person that comes to a different restaurant." Abruptly he leaves the doll corner and heads for his airport in the blocks. As he passes the story table, he says to me, "This is a helicopter restaurant. Not for robbers, not for hunters, not for waitresses."

"Is it only for you?"

"Me and Sarah."

"Sarah? Your baby sister?"

"Me. Only me."

My music room lesson was little more than a pleasant diversion, but the doll corner exercise arouses Jason's initiative

and expands the boundaries of his play. He will not be a hunter
or a waitress; he *will* be a helicopter person in a different
restaurant. So much are his real feelings touched, he is able to
consider the possibility of including Sarah.

The differences in emotional impact between my activities
and the children's are further demonstrated the following day
when a lost-and-found theme in a story of Lilly's explodes into
new play for Jason. "Pawpaw Patch" appears to deal with the
same topic, but her tiny story has the ring of truth.

A little girl is losted. The mother finded her.

"Losted losted losted," Jason echoes, covering up his helicopter. "Finded, finded, finded," he continues, holding it aloft.
Lilly has given Jason usable material.

Jason does not normally say "losted" and "finded." In a story,
shortly thereafter, he says "The helicopter didn't spin higher.
It was lost. Oooo I find it."

But "losted" and "finded" carry more power than my rather
bland pawpaw patch game in which all parts are equally inter-
changeable. Lilly's little girl, lost and recovered, strikes at the
heart of the matter.

Later, Trish questions my interpretation. "Lilly has been telling lost girl stories for months. Why does Jason suddenly in-
corporate the idea into his play and his story? I think 'Pawpaw
Patch' did it."

"You think I push the 'losted-finded' example too far? I just
feel so certain that these emotional references in play and stories far outweigh anything the children find in *our* lessons."

"You mean 'finded.'"

"Ah, yes. Which reminds me, I losted my glasses. Have you
seen them?"

"They're upstairs on the piano. But wait, I've got something
here in my notes I want to ask you about. Did you notice the
children playing library yesterday?"

"Sure I did. It was lovely, the cards, the shelves . . ."

"Alphabetically arranged, by the way. I helped them do it. Did you really like it, Vivian?"

Trish's question surprises me. "Of course I did."

"You didn't tape it."

"Wasn't I taping stories?"

"But you often move the tape recorder when something interesting is going on somewhere else."

"So that's why you think I didn't find the library play interesting?"

"Not in the way you do the straight-out fantasy play."

Gail has been silent until now. "Trish means you don't talk about what Samantha says when she's librarian as much as when she's Jason's mommy."

"Hmm. You have a point there, though surely the library play is a certain kind of fantasy play, isn't it? Aren't they pretending to be grown-up librarians and big schoolchildren?"

"But you didn't tape it," Trish insists. "And you didn't tape the grocery store play or the movers wrapping up the toys in newspaper either."

"You keep track of what I tape?"

"Sure. It tells me what interests you the most."

"Okay, here's a quick answer. Maybe I expect more surprises, more things I can't anticipate, more secrets revealed as the plot—and the camouflage—thickens. But, Trish, does this worry you?"

"Yes, it does. Because I think I prefer the other, the real stuff."

"The real stuff?"

"Play that is meant to look as real as possible. I'm more comfortable with a librarian or a moving man than with Wonderwoman and Batman. As a teacher, I find more connections to the children when we're involved together in . . ."

"Non-fiction play? Trish, really, I very much value the library dramas and moving day—and those marvelous facsimilies in the blocks and sand while the gas company was laying new pipes outside. And Joseph at the toll booth and Dana selling cups of water at the juice stand. I do tape this play but, you're right, not nearly as often as the fantasy play that's more similar to the children's storytelling."

"Do the children tell more of those fantasy tales because you like it more?" Gail wonders.

"Or do I like it more because *they* seem to like it more? Because they seem more spontaneous and articulate in the telling of their invented fairy tales."

"Vivian, just tell me one thing, will you? Aren't both kinds of dramatic play equally important?"

"Absolutely. As long as there *are* both kinds. You know, Trish, most teachers do prefer your 'real stuff.' Anyway, here's a question for you: When Jason's helicopter flies into O'Hare and Midway, is it the real stuff or real fantasy?"

"It's real Jason," Gail answers.

"Look, I made a squirrely hole."

I turn sharply at Jason's voice. This is surely his first squirrel hole, yet no one else finds it remarkable but me.

A small group is playing with crates upstairs in the music room and Jason sits in one now. "This is a squirrely hole. I'm going to fall into a squirrely hole."

Around him, the others are playing a rabbit and fox game invented by Samantha.

"Do you see the fox?"

"He's in the dungeon."

"Catch'em in the down down down."

"Eat'em in the yum yum yum."

"Do you see the fox?"

"He's in the dungeon down down down."

"Fox for dinner."

Jason puts a crate over his head. "This is a squirrel hole. I'm going to fall in the squirrel hole."

"Do you want someone to find you in there, Jason?" I ask.

"Someone can't find me. I'm falling in."

This time I retreat. These impasses may be intended for me

alone. He "finded" his helicopter with Lilly's aid and probably prefers to discover for himself what magic exists in Simon's squirrel hole.

"I'm falling in this hole, this squirrel hole, this squirrel *dungeon* hole."

He captures Simon's attention. "Squirrel holes can't be a dungeon, Jason."

"Dungeon hole."

"Here, I'll show you. Put the crate over your head if a fox comes. Quick, here comes the fox. Hurry, Jason, hide."

Jason follows Simon's every move for the next ten minutes. The helicopter is on the piano bench, within sight, but Jason is definitely not a helicopter, and the crate is not turning into a heliport. It is a momentous scene, yet a very ordinary accomplishment.

Indeed, it is precisely in such simple acts that progress is seen. Jason has entered another child's fantasy and allowed himself to be shown what lies inside. And it was Jason's idea. I had been ready to huff and puff and blow Simon over to the squirrel hole, but Jason stopped me. His "someone" is meant for me. He knows the children's names and will use them when he is ready to face the consequences.

I'm glad Jason has tried out the squirrel hole, but I'd be sorry to see him give up the helicopter house. It is such a good place to learn about school, better even than the story room, I have to admit.

Whatever prevents Jason from full participation in group play is likely to be touched on in the block area. It is here that he can examine the natural rhythm of play while keeping his private base intact. Block boundaries are carefully laid out, and negotiations for space and materials are continuous and exacting.

"That's dangerous, Jason, don't walk over there," Alex orders.

"Yeah, keep away. That's the marsh way. I'm going the marsh way," Joseph cautions, referring to a scene in a book we just read. "It's not for you, Jason."

"Can I go the marsh way?" Eli asks Joseph.

"Yeah, but it's dangerous for helicopters. They'll get stuck. Don't go there, Jason! You're breaking up the marsh way!"

Jason has accidentally dislodged the "marsh way" as he goes to get more blocks. "I could take this house down," he says, pointing to an empty structure.

"You're breaking the marsh way!"

"Get out, Jason!"

"Don't, it's the marsh way!"

Jason is confused, his eyes beginning to fill. "I'm going there now because . . ." He is trying to be reasonable and offer an explanation. "Because . . . there isn't a . . ."

"No, Jason!" Alex screams, pulling his arm. "You don't even know what school is!"

"Because I want to take it down . . ."

"But we're playing with it. It's the marsh way goes over there to that secret place." Alex is moved by Jason's tears. "See where it goes? Look, I'll show you, okay?"

"Okay, I'll go back." Jason wipes his eyes and looks directly at Alex. "I have to fix my house."

"Now look, Jason." Alex's voice is gentle. "Please don't go by the marsh way again or we'll have to explode you."

"Oh, yeah?" Samantha sticks out her tongue. "Well you can't explode someone that they're not even playing with you that they're playing something different."

"So what, Samantha. We'll blast *you* to pieces!"

"So, I'll be a poo-poo bug," is her retort.

"Hey, Samantha, you wanna see the marsh way? It's not too dangerous. Walk this way and jump across that part. That's the sinking part."

"No, thanks, I'm playing with Jason. Y'wanna be the baby and I'm the mother? I'll get the pillows."

"No." He turns his back to her.

"Okay. Anyway, I'm playing with Katie. Bye-bye."

Samantha *knows* how to play. She calls herself a poo-poo bug to diminish Alex's bravado tactics, and she reminds him of classroom rules in her own show of authority. Nearly everything Samantha does and says ought to demonstrate—eventually—to Jason that *children* control fantasy, not the other way around. *She* will decide to be a poo-poo bug or a mother with a baby, frivolous or serious, as she wishes. And, in all seriousness, she is determined to make Jason her baby. This simple fact probably has more to do with Jason's progress in school than all else together. Her notions about control include Jason; he veers between pleasure and dismay at the daily prospect of being her baby.

"I built my house, teacher," Jason says. "Look at. Isn't this a funny house? It looks like school. Up up up down down down."

Samantha adds one block to Jason's house. "Here's another up for you."

"Don't make it taller! It'll fall down."

"It'll fall on you, baby boo. But I'll bandage you up. Stay there. I'll bring the bandage."

"No, it didn't fall. Don't bandage me! These are the upstairs where real helicopters go. Pshshsh."

"Mush mush mush little baby. Here's your bed."

"No! Don't move that block."

"It's okay," she placates him. "I fixed it, little baby."

"No, you twisted it around. The helicopter is broken."

"This is your mother. Look at me. Your mother is here."

Jason smiles in spite of himself. "Wah wah wah," he cries. "Ba ba ba ba."

"You can't talk yet pretend. Okay, little baby Jason? C'mon sweet thing."

He watches Samantha a moment longer, then jumps up. "I don't . . . I'm not . . . you *derailed* me. I'm *derailed* today. That's broken. That's not a baby. Don't take my hand. I'm dee-ray-uld!"

Listening to Jason protect himself, I remember two scenes from his first week of school. In one, Jason sits on the floor with his father, building with Legos. He looks up as I enter the room and his large dark eyes are not welcoming.

"What are you making, Jason?"

"Don't have a conversation with me," he whines. His father smiles apologetically, and Jason moves to block the view.

Another scene takes place at the painting table. This time Jason's mother sits behind him as he paints. Eli points to Jason's helicopter and asks, "Can it fly?"

"Don't talk to me about that!" Jason shouts, frightening Eli with his unexpected intensity.

"Wait, Eli, you didn't do anything wrong," I say, putting an arm around him. "Jason, it's okay if Eli talks to you. That's what happens in school. Eli was being friendly."

Jason stays close to his mother, moving his helicopter around her, landing it on her lap, her shoes, on top of her purse, as he watches us. Surprisingly, the next day, he allows her to leave. He has decided to stay. He and his helicopter.

A few days later, Eli tells me, "Guess what, teacher. Jason let me talk to him."

"I'm glad you told me that, Eli."

"I wanted to see his helicopter and he let me see it but not to touch it."

"I wonder why."

"Because the blade was broken. He was fixing it."

My first conversation with Jason is based on Eli's report. "Jason, Eli told me some good news. He talked to you and you didn't say 'Don't talk to me.' You told him your helicopter was broken. Did you fix it?"

"Yes. But nobody can touch it. It's de-li-cate."

"Okay. I'll tell everyone. Boys and girls, listen. Jason doesn't want anyone to touch his helicopter. It's delicate."

"Br-r-r-ah-ow!" His roar blots out my voice.

Such is the stuff of which school introductions are made, and each child enters through a different door. That Jason has flown in by helicopter is a valuable reminder of the indomitable nature of the human spirit. Those of us who presume to "teach" must not imagine that we know how each student begins to learn.

The story room is small. It must have been a child's room when this school building was a private home. Yet I like acting our stories in such a little area. There is an intimacy that encourages attentiveness, harder to achieve in a large room. And even with twenty-four children, three teachers, and occasional visitors, all seated on low benches around the taped stage, the room has not seemed too small until today.

"Why does it seem so crowded in here?" I wonder aloud.

"Too many people came to storytime, that's why," Lilly says, hugging her large Christmas bear.

"We always have this many, Lilly," I point out. "And there aren't any visitors."

"Because Simon is too close to me," Alex says.

"Maybe he just seems too close because the room looks so crowded. Do you think it's because nearly all of you are holding big toys or stuffed animals?"

"Or Barbies," Joseph tells Samantha.

"I need Barbie or she might get lost. Joseph has a castle. That's too big."

"I need this for He-Man. He's in my story."

"But look," I say, in my complaining voice. "All these things are taking up too much space. How about if we leave them in the other room just when we act out the stories?"

The children look aghast. My idea would replace a dependable old rule that says you may bring anything with you anyplace as long as it doesn't create a problem for others. Is the teacher included in "others"?

"No! That's not a good idea!" Samantha is adamant. "I need Barbie in my story. And it isn't even very crowded."

"You didn't tell a Barbie story," I remind her.

"She's in there. I forgot to say it." In desperation, she puts her Barbie into a three pigs story.

"Tell people to bring *one small* thing," Edward says, examining his tiny Superman figure.

"No fair!" Arlene argues. "My baby wants her stroller. It's because of Jason. *He's* too crowded."

Jason has been paying no attention to the heated discussion but now he looks up. Unless his name is mentioned—or his helicopter—he seldoms listens to a group encounter. He frowns at Arlene and lowers his helicopter behind the three large blocks he has brought into the room today. When did he increase the size to three blocks? I wonder. We are suddenly all aware of the three spaces taken up by the heliport.

"Would you mind terribly, Jason, if you sat on a bench like the others? And you can hold your helicopter on your lap?"

"No."

"No, you don't mind?"

"No."

"What I mean is, could you bring those blocks back and see if it seems less crowded in here? The children don't feel crowded. I'm the one who does."

Without hesitation, Jason lifts the block in front of him and returns it to the other room.

"Do you need help?" I call out.

"No, only me."

I have put the problem on a purely personal basis: I am the one who feels crowded. Jason has responded in the same way the children answered his need for the heliport in the first place.

No one mentions the reason the heliport came to be in the story room. Jason sits spinning his blades, intermittently watching the action on the stage. The others do the same, holding their toys, whispering to one another, looking at books, and, when asked, taking roles in the stories.

It is, after all, unnecessary to concentrate on only one thing at a time. The rhythm of children's thinking doesn't work that way. In play they dig down and under, circle above and around, changing voices and costumes and even playmates when required. Then they return to a problem and pick up where they left off. Jason too can spin his blades, roar, land, break apart, and listen to us, all at the same time.

The next day, perhaps because Jason needs to test out the new arrangement, he flies into Simon's squirrel story but leaves before anyone can say a word. No one thinks about bringing back the heliport, not even Jason. That was one way of solving this diminishing problem. It worked for a while and then created problems of its own.

This is nearly always the way. Problems are not meant to be solved. They are ours to practice on, to explore the possibilities with, to help us study cause and effect. Important issues can't be *solved* with one grand plan—or in one school year. Some are worked at for a lifetime, returning in different disguises, requiring fresh insights.

Play itself is the practicing of problems, a fact demonstrated by even the most casual attention to the passing dialogue.

"The monster is coming! He's almost here!"

"Get the magic belt! When you put it on, he gets froze!"

New conflicts arise everywhere; it is our business to find the magic belt if we can. Solving complaints and eradicating dangers give us a great surge of power and communal purposefulness.

It is the process, not the solution, that conveys the message: There is always a new scenario out there, and we care enough to try to find it.

But must we spend so much time on one child's affairs that it practically fills a book (as I have done with Jason)? Fortunately, the children themselves come to the rescue; each child in turn demands equal time, and every story helps to write all the others.

Alex, for example, is angry lately because he *never*, he says, sits next to Joseph. Simon and Petey *always* do, and it does no good to point out the number of times his wish comes true. More and more of our group times are delayed while Alex refuses to sit down if he can't be next to Joseph.

Jason, by the way, never runs into the stage or discovers that his helicopter is broken while Alex is crying. There seems to be room for only one crisis at a time.

"I had that seat first!" Alex screams, trying to dislodge first Simon, then Petey.

"Wait, Alex. You can't pull people off their seats. Ask them if they'll move."

All three boys shake their heads. "Then I hate this school! I'm not doing anything! I'm not being in anybody's story!" Alex runs out of the room and then returns to stand in the doorway.

The children observe the scene more sympathetically than I do. This is the fourth day Alex has fought over a seat, in the story room, at snack, at music, even at the story table.

"And no one's going to be ever in my story again!"

"Alex is really upset. Does anyone have a suggestion?"

"Let him have a heliport," Arlene says.

"I'm not a helicopter."

"Tell Joseph to move."

"No, I don't want to move."

"Bring a chair and let Alex be in front of Joseph."

"Then I can't see!" Joseph complains.

"Alex can shrink."

"I don't like to shrink."

"Hide and seek," Jason says.

"Is that something Alex can do?" I ask Jason. "Or are you just remembering that game?" There is no reply.

"I gotta idea," Simon says. "Sit on the floor in front of Joseph. Then he'll see over you."

"Hide and seek and peek," Jason adds.

"Ah, *peek* over Alex. That's very helpful, Jason. And Simon, too." I am conscious of feeling a new respect for Jason.

"Okay." Alex accepts the idea, and we all relax. He sits between Joseph's legs, satisfied.

Yesterday's solution involved Alex sitting in the doorway,

and the day before he agreed to sit on my lap. In any case, all selections are purely symbolic because, as soon as he takes a role in someone's story or acts out his own, he takes any available empty seat without comment. He wants confirmation that his needs are important enough to stop the passing parade. These moments of panic in one child or another are activated throughout the day, and the attention they receive gives testimony to the integrity and safety of school life more than any other teacher behavior.

At snack time I bring up the matter of seating preferences. The subject is important, for every child eventually will act out the question: Can I force people to give me the seat I want?

"Joseph, how can Alex solve his problem? He keeps wanting to sit next to you at story time."

"I could save him a seat."

"Simon and Petey, would you mind if sometimes Joseph does that?"

"Then I'll save Petey a seat," Simon decides.

"Save me a seat too," Katie urges.

"You know something, children? I didn't used to allow children to save seats."

"Why?"

"Maybe because when I was little my teachers never let us do it. But once I mentioned this to Miss Silverman, you know, the teacher in Unit 4? And she laughed at me."

"Why did she laugh?"

"She said, 'You always save me a seat at teachers' meetings. Or I save you one if I get there first.'"

The children are silent for a while, thinking about my story. Then, one by one, they begin to laugh, and I laugh with them. It seems to all of us that I've told a good joke on myself.

"You were silly, right?"

"Right. I was telling the children not to do something that I was doing myself."

"Then you never told us again, right?"

"I hope not. If I forget, just remind me."

I wonder if I've achieved the 85 percent positive response Fritz urged upon me years ago. I still find ample evidence of my own misplaced impatience.

For example, Joseph dictates a complicated dinosaur story that elicits a good deal of questioning from me, and later, in the blocks, I pounce on a messier version of the same story like a peevish dragon.

The matter is not unimportant because the spontaneously played out drama clarifies a difficult concept for Joseph that the printed story could not.

> The dragon got two heads. Then a big old old
> dragon comes. Then the baby was first and the baby
> got killed. The other baby. I'm the dinosaur boy,
> then I'm the grandpa dinosaur.

"Are there two baby dragons?" I ask.

"No. First he's a baby then he got old. The dad. Then I growed up. Me and the dad and the grandpa kill the dragon."

"Are you the grandpa or the boy?"

"I'm still the boy but, don't you know, I growed up." Joseph cannot complete the generational separation in his narrative but, moments later, in play, he manages the transition.

"Pretend we kill the dragon, Alex."

"Am I the dad?"

"Yeah. I'm the brother and then I'm the grandfather. That's the king of the dinosaurs because the boy growed huge. Then I was the boy."

"Am I the dad always?" Alex asks.

"Yeah, but first I'm the brother because the dad and the brother killed the dragon that was a baby and then he comes alive again and . . . and . . . that means I'm old . . . first we gotta make the dragon come alive again and first I'm before that the brother."

The boys keep adding blocks to the dragon's tail until it reaches the story table. "Longer! Fire! Pretend the fire comes out over here! Yow! Freezing hot! Longer, he's growing alive! Grandpa! That's me. Don't worry. I'm alive here. Break him down! Kill him dead dead dead!"

Enter the teacher. I ask no questions but instead issue complaints. "Boys! Will you look at that mess! No one can walk there." The logic of play meets adult petulance.

At home, listening to the play sequence on tape I am further disappointed in myself. The concept of boy and grandfather—past, present, and future—comes across more confidently in the block play than on the story paper.

Jason has been observing the drama with unusual interest. As the boys begin to put away the blocks, Jason says, "Bad guy." He is looking at Joseph.

"No I'm not, Jason."

"Bad guy."

"Jason, do you say that because I was angry about the mess they made?" I ask.

Suddenly, Jason knocks over his heliport, then runs to an empty structure and flattens that as well. Clearly he is acting out the dragon scene. I feel certain he is waiting for me to repeat what I said to Joseph and Alex.

"Jason! Look at that mess. The whole floor is covered. No one can walk there."

He looks satisfied. "It bombed up to the sky. Thunder and lightning came."

"Well, as long as I'm helping Joseph and Alex, I'll help you too, Jason. Come on, let's put away these blocks."

"Am I bad?" he asks.

"No. You and Joseph and Alex are good. And you're good block cleaner-uppers."

"Sarah is a bad guy," he says softly.

"Who's Sarah?" Alex wants to know.

"She spits up."

"Your baby?"

"Nobody's baby."

There is no more information forthcoming about Sarah. Jason knocks over the remaining heliport wall and begins picking up blocks immediately. "I'm playing this story," he says, stooping to pick up the blocks. "That guy was bad. Bad crash, bad crash, spank the bad crash."

Is Jason's helicopter fantasy all about being bad? The bad helicopter enters the stage and everyone chases him out; then Jason fixes the blades and the helicopter is good. Being good is safer. Perhaps Jason keeps rebuilding his airport, the way Simon does the squirrel hole, as a confirmation of safety.

"Help! There's a crash over there!" Simon alerts Joseph. "Close the chimney!" Simon's squirrel hole is damaged; Jason's helicopter is broken; Lilly's baby is lost. The differences may be in frequency and style, not in meaning. Jason's way of studying an idea requires many repetitions of a single behavior. He identifies minute errors so he can act them out on a daily basis.

"Mistake" is a word he uses often. "That's a mistake, that's a mistake, and that's a mistake," he says as he draws or paints his pile of helicopter pictures. "Now this one isn't broken. No mistakes." He carries away the perfect picture.

"Are you saving the others, Jason?"

"They have a mistake."

All the pictures look identical to me. "May I see the one you're holding? I'd like to see the mistakes."

We place the pictures side by side. "Show me the mistakes, Jason."

He waves a finger above each picture. "There and there and there, mistake and mistake and mistake." He is acting out "mistake." Break down and repair; mess up and correct; knock apart and rebuild. Bad crash and all, it looks more like thoughtful practice than random damage.

This trial and error method can work well only in a classroom that avoids punishment as a learning tool. Jason and the others are free to experience good and bad, sense and nonsense, without a punitive finale. Harmful acts are stopped, of course, but the absence of "or else . . ." means that the children and I can use one another's mistakes and misunderstandings as lessons in cause and effect.

Most of our errors, teachers' and childrens' alike, are errors in judgment. I have made many but none so serious, in my view, as the long ago "time-out chair." I, who never would have put a dunce cap on a child or put someone in a corner, nonetheless have used this alternate means of removing children from an area of conflict in order for them to "think" about their misbehavior. The fact that the same children always sat on the chair did not make *me* think about its effectiveness.

I repeated my illogical behavior far more often than Jason has flown his helicopter off course, but we both stopped our unrewarding intrusions only when we began to listen to the children's stories. Drama will always replace purposelessness if given a chance.

How could "locking up" a child, even in a centrally located chair, be a substitute for reason and discourse? The image of being locked up is a common fantasy in story and play, but there, at least, the element of personal control, social growth, and intellectual stimulation are possible outcomes. My chair offered silence, anger, and no way out. A child can no more think about social behavior in the abstract than I can teach in the abstract. Children "think" by continuing to play and develop new roles; teachers "think" by observing the ways in which each child moves out of an untenable position and begins to make sense of the classroom.

"Get that kid!" Alex screams at Jason. "Tie him in chairs. He-Man! That kid broke our castle!"

"Police 9-1-1! Calling He-Man police. There's a robber here!"

"My blade is broken," Jason whimpers, surveying the jumble he has created of Alex's building. "I'm fixing my blades."

"Police 9-1-1. Robber fixing blades on 84. Do-not-break-this-again-or-you-will-be-in-jail-for-a-hun-dred-miles."

"Okay," Jason calls out from inside the heliport.

How would the time-out chair have improved the scene? Jason's unexplained destructiveness was incorporated into the drama, and a sensible solution was found by Alex, who himself frequently benefits from this sort of dramatic logic. The time-out chair cannot compete with being in jail for "a hundred miles." Teachers ought not rush in to put robbers in jail; we can safely allow the experts in fantasy to write the script, while we look for opportunities to discuss the outcome.

Gail and Trish bring up a topic we've discussed before: They do not feel authoritative enough without the option of punishment for consistent misbehavior.

"It frustrates you too much?" I ask.

"Absolutely," Gail replies. "You seem to make it work. You're an experienced teacher. When I'm in a classroom by myself, I really think I'm going to need some sort of final threat to hold over a child's head."

"It makes me feel too powerless," Trish adds. "Even now."

"Okay. But I'll tell you this. Once you threaten and punish, the teaching game changes. Difficult children and perplexing situations are no longer looked upon as problems to solve; you create instead the usual classroom story in which punishment becomes a central issue in the drama. Teachers announce it, children respond to it. I'm sorry. I really do think that punishing young children for what they have not yet learned, about social behavior or anything else, is completely counterproductive. It creates *no useful dialogue*." One glance at my colleagues reveals to me that I have not resolved their doubts.

These discussions with Gail and Trish often have the effect of sending me back into time, remembering how it was when I was a young teacher. I felt as they did then, that I could not teach without the "final threat." The time-out chair, my punishment of choice, seemed impossible to eliminate, until the inarticulate sadness of the chair's occupants finally began to penetrate my consciousness.

Looking through old school diaries I find many notations about these dispiriting events. "Charles always sits sideways in the time-out chair" is one comment. "He burrows his chin into his fist and blinks back tears." On the other page, I squirm as I describe his mood. "He looks so disappointed. Yes, disappointed is the word. In himself or in me? Moments earlier he was Luke Skywalker."

Surely there was more logic to Luke than to the chair, but I wrote nothing about that. His impulsive chasing at least offered the advantage of plot and character. My chair was an admission of defeat. What if the principal had ordered me out of the blocks to think about its pitfalls until the children played more constructively?

"I'm sorry you have to sit here again, Charles," I apologized dozens of times, "but you must remember not to push people, will you?"

Charles did not remember. Being locked up seldom helped a child not do something, though it did notify everyone that the child was bad. I had proof of this the day the chair was missing.

"Where's the blue chair?" Ellen asked.

"Mr. Jackson is fixing it."

"Then nobody will be bad today," she reasoned.

"If there's no time-out chair nobody will be bad?" I repeated, wanting to make sure I understood.

"Of course not. How could there be?"

Yet I continued to use the chair. And even when Fritz, that graduate student who did research in my room, showed me on his charts that Charles was not "worst behaved," I still found reason to put him in the chair. It would be five more years before I decided it might be possible to teach without some form of punishment.

Then, one year, in a class I considered exceptionally difficult, I gave up the chair. Abruptly. Unequivocally.

"We're not using the time-out chair anymore," I announced.

The children were startled. They stared at the blue chair, unbelieving.

"Why not?" William asked.

"Because it doesn't do any good. I've been watching carefully. No one behaves any better after being in the chair."

"I do," William insisted.

"But the next day you're in the chair again," I pointed out.

"Then I get good again," he explained. Was the most often "jailed child" afraid of losing his jailer?

"No, I've made up my mind. You'll all have to learn to act properly without the time-out chair. In fact, without any punishment at all. I'm tired of punishing people. It makes children sad and it makes me sad too."

"How will William be good?" Jilly wondered.

"We'll just talk about things," I said. "And, by the way, William's not the only one who sits in the chair." But everyone knew he sat there the most.

The chair labeled him, in my eyes, in the children's, and, worst of all, in his own. I felt a sudden wave of relief. The chair had become a useless and possibly damaging ritual.

I never resumed the practice, but it took a while to fill the void. Shunning the role of punisher did not automatically confer upon me the mantle of dialectician. My desire for useful discourse often turned to recrimination.

"You can't go pushing and stomping like that, William. Look, you made Marni cry and you knocked over all her dishes!"

"I'm an angry wolf," he growled.

"Then be somebody else," I snapped. "You're spoiling everyone's play."

This was hardly a useful exchange, yet without the time-out chair play could continue. And I could better observe the way childen think. When punishment was not an issue, energies pulsated along more creative paths. William's playmates were willing to examine the logic of his behavior and extend the fantasy.

"There's no chimney in this house, William," Marni advised, "so a wolf can't come in."

"Hey, pretend I'm angry because I found out you don't have a chimney and then you forget and you really do . . ."

"But the good witch . . ."

"No, she's a bad witch but . . ."

"No, she's really a good *wolf!* She's your mother wolf, William!"

"No mother wolf! A angry wolf don't gots a mother. Gr-r-r-r!"

"Teacher, William's doing it again! He's being bad."

Perhaps so, but I no longer had to decide if William's behavior was punishable. Instead, I was listening to the plot. I was more curious about his reasoning and less worried about his behavior. Now, after telling him to stop bothering Marni, I was able to ask:

"Why can't an angry wolf have a mother?"

"Mothers aren't in the forest. They're in the den," he answered soberly.

"When you're in the den you're not angry?"

"Only in the forest is where I'm angry."

"And not in houses," Marni adds. "I'm a different mother in a house."

"Could a different mother in a house give food to an angry wolf?" I asked.

"If he doesn't growl," she replied.

These were questions of appropriateness and logic, and before we were done new plans were evolving. The classroom was becoming for me a far more interesting world as I discovered that the child's path to reasonable behavior often was best approached in the form of make-believe. Dramatic necessity and friendship offered better reasons to behave agreeably than some obscure adult purpose in the shape of a chair.

The choice was mine: I could view misbehavior as "bad" and therefore punishable, or consider these unwanted acts to be the misreading of a script-in-progress, awkward stage business that needed reworking. We don't fire the actors just because the early rehearsals are unwieldy. We analyze the script to bring out its inherent logic and to improve the acting.

This notion of viewing misbehavior as poor stage acting appealed to me. Why not create my own stories in which to suggest alterations in behavior? Certainly William needed another perspective in the doll corner.

"William, could you pretend to be a wolf that doesn't knock things over? 'Once upon a time there was an angry wolf and his wolf mother was far away in the den but a different mother let him in and he didn't growl . . '"

"Angry wolfs always growl, you know."

"I know, but, since this mother doesn't like it, where else can you do it?"

Another time I came across William rocking Marni's doll and commented, "This reminds me of that book I read yesterday, *Corduroy*, remember? You're as kind to that baby as Lisa in the book is to the toy bear."

Such experiments in story telling seemed promising. I was searching for new ways to think about behavior and its discontents. Having given up the time-out chair, I needed to replace it with a consistent and positive teaching strategy. It was not enough to view misbehavior as an error in judgment. The question was: How could these errors be used as legitimate learning experiences? I wanted to exchange negative images for positive active roles whenever possible.

"William, you've really upset Tim. Look at him crying. But he'll not feel better if I'm mean to you, so I'll be nice to you both. Then perhaps you'll be nice to Tim also."

It had become clear to me that I could no longer place disruptive behavior outside and in opposition to the main business of the classroom; all accompanying behavior was, in fact, part of the lesson. More accurately, the lesson was part of the continuing life in the classroom, a life as real as the one at home, with problems of equal human dimension deserving the best of our combined concentration. The chair, in its negativism and passivity, was a non sequitur.

Something else was becoming clear to me, and it had much to do with the golden rule I had been told about in childhood but had not often thought of in my own classroom as a teacher: I must not do to a child that which I would not have done to me. As my teaching errors have not been punishable by isolation, humiliation, and denial of activity, I would not impose these sentences upon the children.

Furthermore, just as I expect to be given the benefit of all doubt, so will I attempt to favor the children. For what if I'm wrong and my perceptions are faulty? Was I not mistaken in my assessment of Charles? The implication of Fritz's research in my room did not become immediately clear to me, yet there have been few more convincing demonstrations of my fallibility, and I cannot allow myself to forget.

"Tomorrow is Eli's birthday."

"How old is he?" Lilly asks me.

Eli holds up four fingers. "I'll be tall."

"I'm tall already," Alex says. "Four tall."

"My sister is five," Katie boasts.

Eli wants the spotlight returned to him. "I'm stronger now. I'll turn into a hunter."

"Eli, you have to be bigger to do that," Alex cautions. "When you're a dad or a teenager."

"I saw a helicopter you had to be outside to fly," Jason says.

Is this a non sequitur? Or is Jason thinking about the things bigger people can do? I treat his comment as if it is not off the subject.

"Do you have to be a dad or a teenager to fly that kind, Jason?"

"I saw a helicopter very, very, very high that you have to be outside to fly."

Jason seldom responds, in casual conversation or more formal discussion, to the subject at hand.During play, however, he is definitely advancing in this skill. How can the least structured activity, for which there is no primer or printed curriculum, promise the greatest practice in concentration on a subject? The answer, of course, is that fantasy play is *not* the least structured activity, though the structure is not provided by the teacher. The children are using the most reliable structure ever invented for thinking about anything: story.

Jason has ignored all conversation about Eli's birthday and, at the celebration itself, speaks only of his helicopter. But the next day, in the doll corner, Jason gives a series of relevant responses within the structure of a birthday scene.

"Pretend it's baby bear's birthday, Eli," Lilly says. "You're baby bear. Pretend someone stole your bears and then someone finded your bears and it's your birthday."

"I stealed them back for you," Jason says.

"Who are you, Jason?" Lilly asks.

"I found your bear."

"Oh, come in, come in. Look, father, this is someone that finded our bear in the woods from the monster."

"Not from a monster. The bear was lost in the woods. I was walking there."

"To pick blueberries for baby bear's birthday?"

"Here's the blueberries," Jason says, giving Lilly some play-dough. He sits down in a rocking chair, helicopter in hand, rocking and humming along with Lilly. Soon Eli joins the humming. They are all serious students of the same subject: No one is off task.

The dictated stories give me my best opportunity to help children organize their ideas within a designated framework, but in play the children themselves initiate the process. Jason is learning to focus on someone else's subject and add to its development. He does not manage this too well in conversation or storytelling, but when he plays he takes a flying leap forward.

"This is a helicopter house," Jason announces. "It's not standing up, it's not falling . . ."

"Well, don't put your helicopter on mine," Edward responds.

"Bing bing bing. Listen to my blades, Edward."

"I can't hear them. My windows are closed."

Jason examines Edward's building from top to bottom. "It's too high up," he says. "People in there will get hurt."

"There's bears in here, Jason."

"Bears and people will get hurt. Hey look, my helicopter can move. Over your bear house. It flew over." Jason has not left his helicopter house but he pretends he's flying over Edward. "Oooooo it's going all over your house. Open your windows."

"Yeah, I see it," Edward says.

"You heard it zoom zoom zoom over your house?"

"No, I didn't hear it Jason, because the windows are closed."

"I think someone opened your window."

"Yeah, they did. I heered the helicopter."

There are times when I pretend to be busy, rolling up paintings or cutting scraps for the pasting box, but I am really *listening*, allowing the waves of fantasy to wash over me.

Samantha and Joseph rush in from the playground, waving little twigs. They are bursting with inspiration; I can't wait to see what story they are about to play out, especially since I have at least twenty minutes left on my tape cassette.

"Pshush! Turn to one sword! Two swords can turn to one sword. One sword can turn to a hundred swords."

"Save me, Superman! Turn my sword into a hundred rainbows."

"Okay. There! The hundred rainbows. Now I turned them into a hundred arrows until God."

Their unrehearsed poetry is astonishing. Only in play can they climb so high and see so far, and Jason is as much a poet as anyone. He comes in from the playground to use the toilet and stops in the doorway.

"Hi, Jason," Samantha says. "You can be the rainbow baby. Joseph is the dad."

"I can't. I have to go back outside."

"Why do you?"

"Because I'm running back and forth as fast as the sky and faster than the clouds."

"Are you pretending to be a helicopter?" I ask.

"No, a real helicopter."

"Real pretend?"

"No, only just a helicopter."

Our abstractions carry us no further. To find out more I must listen to the children play.

In the morning, Jason begins a new study. When I describe it later to Gail and Trish I call it "determined ambivalence."

"My story is in my house," he says. "No, it's not in my house." He sits in his helicopter house and purposely initiates a dilemma.

"Do you mean you want to tell a story about your helicopter house?" I ask.

"No. Yes. No, I want to."

"Should I put you on the list?"

"No. My story is in my house."

Samantha intercedes. "He means he wants to stay in his house and tell his story."

"No. Yes."

"You're having a hard time deciding, Jason. I'll ask you again later."

The incident attracts Simon's curiosity. He decides to test Jason's strategy. "Can I come in, Jason?"

"Yes. No, I want to play alone."

"You said yes?" Simon asks.

"Yes, no, I want to play alone."

"Do you want me to play with you?"

"Yes . . . no."

"Anyway," Simon says slowly. "I'm playing with Joseph so I can't come in. Here, put this over there for a helicopter fuel pump." He hands Jason a wooden cylinder and runs off, and Jason places the unexpected gift next to his helicopter. "Pshush. Yes no yes no go in go out pshush." He drops the cylinder outside.

To be or not to be, to give or not to give. This seems to be on Jason's mind at snack as well. "I do want raisins," he says, taking a handful, "but I don't want them," giving them back.

"Jason, do you want the raisins or not?"

He grabs another handful and then quickly empties the raisins into my hand. "Yes no." He is not smiling.

What is this all about, I wonder. Is he acting out his uncertainty about school—or simply teasing us? In either case, of course, he finds himself with no friend in his house or raisins in his hand.

Gail and Trish think it's funny. "He's acting out that good ol' cliche': mixed messages," Gail laughs.

"You think I'm making too much of this?" I ask.

"Well, isn't it possible he's just having some fun? Maybe it's a game they play at home."

"Or maybe he *is* acting out the idea of mixed messages—and *I'm* the one who plays that game he's curious about."

"What do you mean?"

"Well, it seems to me I do more of that where Jason is concerned than with anyone else. Here's a good example: Yesterday Jason momentarily rested his helicopter on Simon's squirrel house. Now I know how eager Simon has been to include the helicopter in his squirrel play, so I said something like, 'I see your helicopter is playing in the squirrely hole.' Both boys were surprised because it obviously wasn't so. Then I tried to get out of *my* hole by saying, 'I mean, it *looks* as if it is.'"

Gail smiles at me. "So Jason is wondering what *your* game is?"

"Well, why would I pretend he's playing with Simon when he isn't?"

"Yeah, it's a bit like Jason—do you remember?—telling Simon he's outside the window when he wasn't," Trish says.

"Exactly. And here's the teacher doing it. Can you trifle with people in such ways or can't you?"

I struggle with these paradoxes, and so does Jason. He continues to act out his inquiries until he feels satisfied. "My story is in my house," he tells me again, a day later.

"You're playing in your house?" I ask.

"My *story* is playing in my house."

"Not on paper," I suggest. I am no longer impatient; I am truly curious. Now I will be at my best. "Not yet on paper, Jason? But when you sit next to me at the story table, you'll take the story that's in your house and we'll put it on paper?"

"Without words," he replies.

"Oh, with*out* words. You want to tell me the story but you don't want me to write it down."

"He means the kind I did that time, remember?" Simon explains.

"Jason, are you thinking about a story while you're playing in your house and you want to act it out at story time without first putting it down on paper? The way Simon did a few days ago?"

"Yes. No."

"But maybe?"

"Yes. That's what he means," Simon assures me.

It doesn't matter if we have figured out Jason's meaning. Simon and I have treated the subject with the seriousness it deserves. We are using Jason's behavior as an exercise in logic and Jason follows along. Multiply the effect by twenty-four children, one hundred and eighty school days a year, and you have an intensive continuous curriculum in language and thought. Take away the play and storytelling, however, and the subject matter is meager and unimaginative.

"I want to sit *here*," Jason says as we settle down in the story room.

"No, don't sit by me!" Alex insists, moving alongside Samantha who quickly occupies the seat he has just left.

"I don't want you, Samantha," Jason says, capturing the empty seat next to Alex, and this time Alex doesn't object. All these yesses and nos happen so fast I have no time to respond, but it is clear that the children consider these behaviors logical and socially correct.

Alex's story of the day treats the yes-no issue in dramatic

form. Having listened to an irreverent three pigs story told by Samantha, he immediately creates a literary yes to her no. Here is Samantha's version:

> Once upon a time there lived three little pigs. And then came a big bad wolf. And the little pigs got ate up by the big bad wolf. And then they got ate up by all the big bad wolfs. Happily ever after.

Alex responds sharply:

> Those pigs. The big bad wolf eated them but he had a gun inside his stomach and the pigs shooted him apart. Then they boiled him for supper. Happily every after.

I watch Samantha's three pigs being "ate up" by the wolves and wonder how this fits in with her need to mother Jason. And where, for that matter, in Alex's confident response is the child who cries because he can't sit next to Joseph?

To the children, the most interesting aspects of the classroom are the vastly different ways people find to behave, even ways that are sometimes disruptive or confusing. Not one child would wish for an end to the helicopter house. Jason's single-minded fantasy is a beacon for the integrity of the individual. And Alex, fierce lion and wolf-eater, must certainly cry if he wants to sit next to Joseph but can't. The children want to know how the teacher meets his demands because they will have similar claims to make at other times.

What shall be done for Alex, who is jealous, and for Jason, who flies into stories? Such questions are among the most valuable ones that can be heard in a classroom. The work of twenty-four children and their teachers as they analyze one another's clashing fantasies and conflicting desires provides training in the highest order of social responsibility and logical thought.

Each time the children explain their own difficulties or help define and solve the problems of others, the curriculum rises like Joseph's hundred arrows and Samantha's hundred rainbows. Perhaps Jason says it best: We run as fast as the sky and faster than the clouds.

Jason is unhappy today, and we don't know why. Perhaps he's coming down with a cold, though his congestion could be the result of so much crying.

It is clear that he doesn't want to be in the story room with us. "You don't have to stay, Jason. Why don't you play out there, in the heliport? Or paint a picture?"

"No! No! I don't want to go out there!" he sobs, running out of the room and returning instantly.

"Then stay with us, why don't you."

"No! I don't want to be in here."

"Someone can keep you company out there." Several hands go up and Samantha is already at his side.

"I don't want company. I'm looking for my helicopter bones," he cries. "They're broken. My helicopter bones are broken!" His face is smeared with tears and mucus. Edward whispers to Eli, "He's going to throw up, watch."

I wipe Jason's face and sit him on my lap. "We'll all be very nice to you, Jason. Tell us what you want us to do." But he is not ready to stop crying and so I continue to wipe away his tears.

"You wanna hold my pound puppy?" Simon offers.

"Let him sit on *my* lap," Samantha says.

"He wants his mommy."

"Do you, Jason? Should we call her?" He shakes his head, still crying, though somewhat less.

"Let him be in all the stories," Joseph says.

"All the stories," Alex echoes. "Put a helicopter in every story."

"Not in mine," Lilly pouts.

"I mean if people want."

Jason stops crying and looks at the children pensively. "Okay," he sighs.

"See, he likes my idea!" Joseph is elated. "That was in my dream, really. I was in everyone's story."

"Were you in mine?" Lilly asks.

"Yeah, I was."

Later, in the blocks, Jason acts out his recurrent daydream. "I'm locked in here. I can't get out. I'm a bad guy." His fantasy has become a game. He wants me to ask, "Who locked you in?"

"You did," he always responds.

"How will the bad guy get out?"

"I've got things to twist around. I got two things to spin. I'm locking me in now so I'll never get out."

Lilly looks worried. "Even when your mother comes?"

"Watch me, Lilly," Jason says. "Look at the bad guy in the bad guy house because I got two things to spin."

"Can I see?"

"You can come in. Push that block because it's a trapdoor. Then move it back."

Lilly follows Jason's directions into the bad guy house. The two children sit quietly, bodies touching in close quarters. "Watch me spin this, Lilly."

"Can I spin it?"

"Okay, but give it back in a short minute."

My mind spins like the helicopter blade. On his unhappiest day, Jason is able, for the first time, to invite another child in to play. He has been angry with us the whole morning, and suddenly he commits himself to Lilly.

The events in the story room were as dramatic as one could imagine in a classroom. Jason cannot stay, yet he cannot leave. He pits himself against the teacher, the children, and even against story time. Everything comes to a halt while Jason cries. The attention paid to the tears of a single child brings the entire group to a higher stage of behavior. The class struggles to find a way out. Then Joseph offers a dream. From no role suddenly come six.

There had been no place for a helicopter in Lilly's story, but she follows him into the blocks and, on his least connected day, becomes his friend. If Jason was crying for no reason, how could the outcome be so good?

One must be in awe of such mysterious unplanned resolutions. Clearly, we do not understand most of what motivates the children.

"Do you want to be the daddy, Jason?"

"This is a bad guy house, Lilly."

"It can't be. There's not a mother lives in a bad guy house."

"Why?"

"Because mothers don't like bad guys."

"Can mothers be in a helicopter house?"

"If they have a pillow." Lilly proceeds to play her second favorite game, furnishing a block house. Her first favorite is still hunting for the lost child. I wonder if Jason will ever join her in that fantasy.

The kitchen and bedroom supplies pile up inside Jason's small enclosure but he has stopped participating. He seems to be listening to Joseph at the story table.

"Mine is a trouble story. Superman comes . . ." Joseph turns to Arlene who is drawing rainbows. "Guess what? Skeletor and Hordak aren't friends anymore. Because this was a good Skeletor."

"I thought Skeletor was only a bad guy," I comment.

"Yeah and there's also a good one too," Joseph assures me.

"Who am I?" Jason calls out.

"Are you the helicopter you mean?" asks Joseph.

"Am I the good or bad one?"

"I don't know." Joseph looks puzzled.

Jason must solve this dilemma himself, in his own time. The answer lies somewhere inside his fantasy but also in every experience he has with friendship and fairness.

This year, fairness seems to include a deep feeling that everyone has the right to behave inconveniently. It is fair for Alex to cry if he cannot sit beside Joseph and equally fair for Jason to cry when he cannot decide whether or not to remain in the story room. It is especially fair for me to pay serious attention to their sorrows.

Decisions about fairness, it seems, often appear as the result of someone's tears. We teachers are not overly fond of crying when there is no physical hurt, but the children insist that crying means something is unfair and needs to be corrected. It is never a case, for them, of the adult "giving in" to tears; on the contrary, the sympathetic adult receives high marks for fairness when tears are respected.

"Pretend you're small, Jason," Samantha says in the doll corner. "Pretend you're not born yet. You have to be fourteen. Then you can be age. First a baby."

Jason sits at the table rolling out playdough, listening to plans that include him. "Here's a rope," Edward tells him, giving him a tie. "Because you're small. You need a rope to climb things. Come in, Jack."

I love to follow these connections made during play. The concept of small leads to the image of rope climbing, which in turn leads to Jack of "Jack and the Beanstalk," who, though small, is powerful like the number 14.

Jason is still thinking about small. "When I stop being a big boy," he says to Samantha, "I'll grow smaller and smaller."

"Until you're a baby again," she says. "Then you'll be my baby. Baby take a nappie, come on, baby. Here's your bottle, baby."

"I'm Jack already," Jason says, leaping out of his chair. "I'm climbing."

"You have to still be the baby, Jason. We're not doing Jack yet."

What will Jason do now? Samantha keeps maneuvering him into the baby role, forcing him to devise new ways to escape. Normally, the helicopter blades would begin to turn, but instead Jason creates another distraction to avoid an unwanted role.

"Soon I'll put water on my head!" he giggles. "Then I'll put a toy on my head and I'll put water on the toy and it'll spill down on my head!" Jason laughs loudly, and the children laugh with him.

"Water on your head pee-pee."

"Pee-pee in your head."

"Wee-wee on your head."

"Poo-poo on my head," Jason says and, as suddenly as the comedy skit began, it is over. I peek in to see if the scatological dialogue has been accompanied by an unacceptable mess, but everyone is peacefully rolling and pounding playdough.

"Hi, teacher," Samantha says. "It's the baby's birthday. She just got borned."

"Who is the baby?"

"Jason. He's a she-baby."

"Are you, Jason?"

"Yes." He smiles shyly and climbs into the crib. "Cover me up, Samantha. So I don't be cold."

When was it decided that Jason should be a she-baby? Reviewing the scene later from the tape, there is no mention of Jason's new identity until I ask "Who is the baby?" However the notion has come about, it is apparently an idea whose time has come.

"You're in my story, Jason," Edward says. Jason is drawing helicopters and doesn't look up.

"I'm putting you in right now. Are you listening?"

"Yes, I'm listening."

Can this be Jason? Surely "I'm listening" must be the most beautiful words a teacher can hear in the classroom, next to "I'm your friend."

"Once there was a boy and he had a bird and the bird was hungry so the boy found some food and gave it to him. The end."

Edward looks at Jason. "Oh yes and there was a helicopter. It flied over." Jason smiles and says, "Y'wanna hear my story? The helicopter flies in the night. Edward is in the airplane."

Jason has glimpsed the reciprocal connections between storytellers: I'll put you in my story, and you put me in yours. How does this understanding come about? The weight of experience must be the main factor in developing this essential component in the learning process. You listen to my idea, and I'll listen to yours.

Every day Jason observes other children repaying role assignments, in stories, play, and conversation. Now he can begin to respond in a similar fashion.

"If that helicopter flies here, Jason, it can land on my runway," Simon promises.

"Pretend it's flying there," Jason says, and Simon is satisfied. Jason has gone further than is usually the case. Simon accepts "pretend" as the deed itself.

My desire for connections must be no greater than Jason's. He has embarked upon an open-ended investigation of the classroom, and each breakthrough propels him to test new possibilities. Yet, no matter how closely I follow his progress, I cannot predict what will follow.

"I'm going to help Ira," he announces. "I'm going to help Ira because he doesn't want any of those kids to help him."

Ira is alone at the sandbox, trying to keep a tunnel from collapsing. "Don't touch the tunnel, Jason."

"He's gonna . . . he wants me to help him. I'm flattening the sand."

"Don't touch the tunnel, Jason."

"Look, Ira. I'm digging a big hole."

"Yeah, that's what I need. Fill that up with water. Hurry up. I need a lake."

Jason runs to me, shaking with excitement. "Where's the water? I need to bring water. Hurry me up!"

"I'll find you a pail, Jason. Let me show you how high to fill it."

"Because I'm doing a big job? You're showing me because I'm helping Ira?"

"Right. If you need more, you can do it yourself."

"If *Ira* needs more. I'm helping Ira," Jason says. "Is he my friend?"

"I think he must be."

"What's the matter, baby?" Jason says, drawing his helicopters. "What's the matter, baby," he continues saying as he brings his pile of drawings into the helicopter house. He has borrowed a line from Arlene's story and nourishes himself as he plays.

Here is Arlene's story:

> There was a big big monster. Then the baby said,
> "Oh, no!" And the daddy said, "What's the matter
> baby?" And the sister said, "What's the matter
> baby?" And the mother said, "What's the matter
> baby?" And they were home.

"What happens to the monster?" Katie asks.

"I told that part."

"So this story is about what everyone says to the baby and nothing more about the monster?" I conclude.

"Right. This is *not* a dream," Arlene replies.

In the story room, the monster remains outside the stage while the baby sleeps, and he returns to his seat the moment the baby wakes up. The monster is the dream itself. Arlene's emphasis on the comforting aftermath of a bad dream produces an immediate hush as we act out her story. Everyone gazes longingly at Arlene, the baby who awakens to such anxious, loving solicitation. It is a moment to be preserved. She has defined love.

"Let's act it out again, Arlene. Can we? And when the baby

wakes up, let everyone ask 'What's the matter, baby?' I think we all want to say that."

We repeat the brief sequence twice and, the second time, Jason joins the chorus. Twirling his blades, he says "What's the matter, baby?" as if he is talking to his helicopter.

Samantha, sitting next to him, jokes, "What's the matter, Jason?"

"Not Jason. You have to say baby," he tells her gravely. "Jason is not the baby."

"Yes you are. In my head you are."

Such are the events that make the classroom a functioning family, sensitive to the emotions and conflicts within each member. To the extent that the teacher plays the good parent, uncovering the urgent issues that connect us, the teaching role is performed well.

We hold the classroom family together as we demonstrate our curiosity about every dream and story, as we worry along with all who complain and all who cry over every new kind of anguish.

We show that Arlene's frightened baby, and Jason's broken blades, and Alex's anxieties about seating, and the integrity of Simon's squirrel hole, and Samantha's need to be Jason's mother, are as important as anything else school has to offer. Learning to know one another, we develop the logical and emotional precedents required for all other studies.

If we in this class are a family, then Jason is most often the barometer of feelings and fulfillment for that family.

"There's a helicopter, not Jason, in my story," Edward says.

"Guess what? Jason let me hold his helicopter," Joseph tells me breathlessly. "I told him he can come to my birthday."

"Jason needs a cape," Samantha worries, realizing he is the only one in the blocks not wearing a cape.

"Drivers don't wear capes, Samantha," Joseph says.

"I'm making him one because he might be lonely," she replies.

Do the children focus this much on Jason because I do? Or

do we watch him—and try to change him—because he reminds us of our own unfulfilled needs? He does have a way of reenacting unresolved conflicts that gives us the opportunity for further study of the issues involved.

"Don't do that, Joseph!" I protest. "Don't let the blocks fall like that. They'll get chipped."

"I didn't!" he argues, staring at the pile at his feet.

"Do-not-let-the-blocks-fall-like-that!" Jason repeats, swooping a shelf of blocks onto the floor. I know what he wants me to do. It is what everyone in the block area wants: to repeat, in the same voice, my words to Joseph.

"Don't do that, Jason! Do not let the blocks fall like that! They'll get chipped."

Satisfied, Jason resumes his helicopter play. Joseph somehow feels validated, and all who witnessed the scene are content. No one else, right now, needs to find out if I am ambivalent about the rule. Nor do they need to worry if someone will get punished for breaking the rule. Every event contains the answer for some child's unasked question.

Today a strange snow blizzard rages at our windows, accompanied by lightning and thunder. The children attempt to take control of the elements as they play and Jason, sitting quietly in his helicopter house, not even twirling his blades, listens to the excited play around him.

"This is my sled. Help! It's breaking to pieces!"

"My sled is blind. It can't see the snow."

"Here, break that blind up."

"Turn on the window wipers. They exploded! We can't see! Because the lightning got us!"

"It's cracking us apart. Superman can't be killed by lightning."

"Spiderman! Over here. Throw a web over that evil snow."

Petey brushes away the web. "Mighty Mouse doesn't need a web. Whoosh! I destroyed the snow."

Jason's heliport is directly adjacent to the window; the storm appears to be lashing out at his building. "Spiderman, over here," he says. "This helicopter doesn't need a web. Whoosh. This blade destroyed the snow."

Finally, Jason's helicopter is given a heroic task. It is well enough, for awhile, to use a symbol to keep people away or to reinforce a comforting pattern of breaking and fixing. But, if you cannot use your symbol eventually as the instrument for effective, powerful control, it will need to be discarded. Jason has been listening to superhero play for months without building connections to his own problems. Suddenly, during a moment of real fear, the message has come across.

The specter of fear overtaking a child in the classroom is an ever present possibility and a complex matter to deal with. Children are said to fear the unknown, but the problems are far more complex than this maxim implies. Children fear certain unknowns and not others; events such as the spring blizzard are easily handled in play and talk, but other incidents that seem of no consequence to the teacher can create an impasse of denial.

For example: Katie is passing out Snoopy stickers, an advertising promotion given to her father at his store. Each one is covered with a paper that must be peeled off to see the picture. As she distributes the cards, we turn the event into a game. "How many different pictures are there?" I ask Katie.

"I don't know."

"How can we find out?"

"Everyone has to open and look," she says.

"Good idea. I'll keep a record on the board. Every time someone finds a new kind I'll draw a quick picture and then I'll put a mark under it when someone else gets the same kind."

Using stick figures I copy Snoopy with Charlie Brown, Snoopy with Lucy, Snoopy with Woodstock, and so on. There is a choice of six by the time Katie arrives at Jason's seat.

"Mine is a helicopter," he says, without peeling the cover off.

"Well, so far all the cards have Snoopy. Could you look inside?"

"Mine is a helicopter."

"Do you want someone else to open it for you?"

"No."

"Okay. Jason is guessing he has a helicopter. I'll draw a helicopter picture. And I'll put a question mark, like this. It means Jason is guessing."

No one thinks Jason's behavior is strange; the children's invented games always include the unexpected exception to the rule. Samantha is an expert at this.

"You get two cards for landing," she had instructed Jason earlier, giving him hastily manufactured squares of paper. "But I get four because my circle is blue." Jason gladly took her card; he is unafraid of a card made by another child.

Adult-manufactured items, however, can contain disagreeable matters. He doesn't want to be surprised by a picture he might not like, a feeling well known to many children. Again I use Samantha as an example, because she appears so confident. Yet, when it comes to surprises in print, she can become suspicious or fearful.

Often when we begin an unfamiliar book, she will stand up and head for the doorway. "Is there a part I won't like?" she'll ask.

"I didn't see any scary parts."

"Did you look at all the pages?"

"Well, there's one page that has a lost puppy on it but he finds his mother pretty soon."

"Don't read that page."

"I'll tell you when I get there, and you can wait in the other room until I turn the page."

Samantha leaves the room and returns quickly, invariably asking me to reread the part she missed. Jason too has peeled off the paper on the Snoopy card as soon as we move to another activity. Both children are attempting to deal with the *anticipation* of fear, more than with fear itself.

By age three and four, children arrive at school with unique lists of unpleasant memories. "Try it, you'll like it" is not, generally, advice that is acceptable on the spot. True, there are always those who seem unafraid of that which is new and untested, but there are far more who hesitate.

To hesitate is *not* to be lost; it means only that you may arrive somewhat later at the same place.

Another milestone. Jason is copying another child's structure without knowing what it is.

"I need crates, I need crates," Jason chants. "Mine has to be like Eli's."

"Here are two more, Jason," I say.

"You're putting them the wrong way, teacher. They're supposed to go this way. Like Eli's."

"What are you making, Eli?" I ask.

"A dinosaur like Joseph did."

"How do you get out?" Lilly wants to know.

"This is the exit. Go down this way."

"Hey, guys, look at *my* exit," Jason calls. "You guys go down here."

Eli leaves his crates and follows Jason's directions, whereupon Jason begins to howl. "No, no! This is mine!"

"But Jason, we just heard you say 'You guys go down here,'" I remind him.

"No! That doesn't mean that. That means something else. And they broke my house. I have to make it again."

This at least is a fairly consistent reaction of Jason's. When he is worried he tells us something is broken. If the situation feels wrong, uncertain, threatening, or simply unfamiliar, he identifies one of a small list of items as broken and proceeds to fix it. It is his way of recovering his equilibrium.

In a way, I try to do the same thing. To be sure, we are not, either of us, reaching down to root causes; we are acting as if the classroom is a separate world in which another kind of sense guides our behavior. We join with the children to set up our own codes of fairness and our own system of security. We say: Let every conflict or misunderstanding be resolved each day according to the rationale of the moment; the next day, we will try again.

This approach makes sense to Jason. He tries out new solutions to old quandaries by watching the ways other children conduct their affairs. Using "exit," he wonders if it will help him feel comfortable inviting people into his structure, but he finds it doesn't quite lead to the feelings he anticipated. Nonetheless, these are giant steps, for he is listening to the children's play.

Jason's biggest problem, as I see it now, is not the helicopter fantasy at all, but rather the fact that he seldom watches the other children. He is beginning to understand that *they* are the ones who can show him the best ways to fix his moods and misgivings within the context of play.

"Awk, awk, awk, we're squirrels. Teacher, teacher, pet us or we can't stop awking." Lilly and Eli are crawling around my feet waiting to be scratched behind their ears. It is an old game we play, but this is the first time Jason really sees what they are doing.

"Okay, little squirrels," I say. "Scratch, scratch, rub-a-dub dub." As soon as I pet each child, the squeaking ends, but a few moments later, the children return, repeating the same pattern. Long ago I learned to go along with such games no matter how often repeated. They are of enormous importance to young children—and even to older students. In the midst of their own intense activity, they may suddenly need the teacher's reassurance, and they invent ways to obtain comfort without stepping too far out of their roles.

Jason begins to mimic "Awk, awk." After a short hesitation, he crawls over to my chair, whispering "Awk, awk, awk, awk." He increases his volume until he is fairly shouting. "Awk! Awk! Awk!"

"Stop, Jason," Katie complains. "You're hurting my ears. Can't you see I'm trying to color?"

"I'll stop if you pet me," he tells her.

"Okay, I'll pet you."

Now Jason returns to me. "Awk! Awk! Awk!"

"I'll pet you too, Jason," I say, rubbing his neck. "Are you a squirrel?"

"I'm a helicopter."

"Oh. I didn't know helicopters like to be petted."

"Sometimes they do."

Jason is borrowing new ideas every day now. The next morning he pushes a cardboard sword down the back of his shirt, murmuring something that sounds like "Ka-wee." He is copying Edward, who has taken to wearing a sword in this fashion without explaining why.

Jason says nothing about the sword when he sits down next to me. "I'm doing everything in music today," he tells me instead. "I'm being just an airplane that does everything."

"So if we do 'Hop Old Squirrel' you'll be an airplane?"

"But not in stories. Only in music."

"You won't fly into people's stories?"

"I'll ask is there a helicopter and is there a sword," he says with great seriousness.

"Because now you have a helicopter and a sword."

"Two things. I have two things. This and this."

Jason regularly proves to me that children adapt best to school through the culture they themselves invent. As I continue to make small forays into their world of play and story, we meet at an increasing number of intersections. I cannot allow myself to think in overgeneralized terms about Jason and his classmates, for these intersections exist mainly within the minutiae of dramatic details.

"Look at my house, teacher," Jason says. "It has all sorts of windows in it. One, two, three, four."

"I helped him make the windows," Ira says.

"Help me again, Ira, 'cause it got broken down."

"I can't, Jason, I'm playing with Samantha. You wanna be the queen again, Samantha?"

"Okay, pretend I'm traveling around in a different place, Ira. Pretend you don't see me yet."

"Pretend you're booming around," Ira tells her.

"Pretend I'm booming around and then I see you and you're the king of the queen." Samantha begins to make herself a crown.

"But you don't know it yet because you're booming around."

Jason has been staring at Ira and Samantha during their entire conversation. "Ira, look at me," he says. "I'm booming around. I'm making a fountain and I'm booming around. It's to boom around with. Hey, teacher, I wanna do my story now." He begins his story on the way to the story table.

> A helicopter is flying higher higher higher booming
> around and booming around. And then it creeped
> down from the sky and then it landed.

"That's two ideas you got from Ira," I point out, but Jason shakes his head. "*Samantha* is booming around. She's a queen. And she's booming around in a different place."

"When does she find the king?" I ask.

"First she's booming around. Then she sees the king."

We converse as if we have just been to the theater together. We now draw from a store of immediate references and allusions; all this because Jason is listening to other children—and so am I.

A major reason why other children are able to provide him with so beneficial a learning environment is that, although they include more people, places, and things in their play, the issues in their play and his are similar.

Jason continually pretends something is wrong and then quickly corrects the problem. Much of everyone's play follows the same formula. Jason defines this aura of vulnerability so well it forms a background for the improvised performances of others. His high-pitched voice, detailing the measures he takes to fix broken helicopters and houses, projects the universal theme for all characters in trouble.

"This chimney is cracked open, teacher," Jason says. "There's something inside there cracking it open. I'll fix it so it won't be cracked open."

Nearby, Edward's roller coaster is veering dangerously off course. "Help, help, this isn't stopping! Ira, Ira, save me. I'm going to crash! Sand bags, sand bags . . . ah ah!"

Under the window seat, a bad hunter approaches a mother and her baby. "Here's your bed, Dana. Lie down."

"Don't go there, mommy! A bad hunter!"

While Jason's accompaniment continues: ". . . my chimney is cracked open. First I take down all these pieces . . ."

And in the opposite corner, some jailed kittens are about to sink into quicksand. "Save me, save me. This is the lion tamer's jail! Quicksand! Grab the magic belt!"

". . . maybe maybe the chimney won't be cracked open again because I'm doing this very slowly and very carefully and I'm not making any mistakes again this time."

Jason completes his house. "There, now this house is locked. Because there's a bad hunter over there." It is no longer possible for Jason to restrict himself to one theme. The play of others beckons to him from all directions, compelling him to try new expressions and act out his losses and gains in a wider variety of ways. He doesn't need to abandon his helicopter, for the children understand its value and encourage its use.

Jason is having an ordinary conversation at the snack table. When did he begin to speak to children in such a natural way?

"I'm going to Florida," Eli says. "On a plane."

"I told Mommy can we go on a trip," Lilly says. "I'll tell her can we go with you."

"Did you see the propellers?" Jason asks. "They're under the wings."

"I didn't see them yet."

"Yeah, you really could see them if you sit down in a propeller plane," Jason advises. "By the window. But not if it's a jumbo jet."

"You're right, Jason," Simon agrees enthusiastically. "You mean a little plane. That kind."

"I'll tell my mother to go on that kind," Eli decides.

"Then you can see the propellers go round and round," Jason concludes.

We have not heard such ordinary talk before from Jason, yet at home he probably converses in this manner all the time. We judge and evaluate Jason in a place where he has not been comfortable enough to engage in good conversations. In school he has felt in need of repairs. I must always assume, with any child, that school is the source of whatever problems exist in school before looking elsewhere.

But what if I am aware of unusual or unhappy home conditions? Especially so then, for now the classroom will have an even greater responsibility for providing a sensible world.

Of course, it is natural to seek blame in other places. The children do it frequently. Edward's roller coaster game is not working well today and, as his frustration mounts, he blames his closest neighbor.

"Stupid Jason! Stupid, stupid!"

"Why are you yelling at Jason?"

"He's making too much noise. I can't remember how to do this damn thing."

"Are you making noise, Jason?"

"No."

"Then it must be another reason, Edward. Can I help?"

"I'm not doing this damn thing anymore!"

He kicks the track apart angrily. "You know why I'm so mad? Because Joseph wouldn't sit next to me before."

"A long time ago?"

"Yeah, that time. I'm really mad!"

"Well, here's my advice. Think of something that makes you feel good and do it."

"I'll paint. No, I'll do a story." He puts "bad" into his story five times.

> There's a bad lion. He broke the clock because it was
> a bad clock. He broke the track because it was a bad

track. Then he saw a kitty. 'You're a bad lion.' 'No I'm not bad.' Happily ever after.

Why is Edward in such a bad mood? There is much going on at home that makes life difficult for him and other family members—and the family is receiving help from outside sources. Nonetheless, it is possible to view nearly everything that happens in the classroom within the context of life in the classroom. Each action may be examined by the individual, group, and teacher in terms of what we see and hear, providing that our consistent *stated* goal is to see and hear and talk about everything that happens—and try to find a fair solution.

Perhaps in response to Edward's unwarranted attack, Jason has been upset all morning. Nothing is right, he calls everything a mistake. At snack, his empty juice glass provides the reason for all that is wrong in this classroom.

He sobs loudly. "I need my juice, I need my juice, you didn't fill it up."

"I'll be ready in a moment, Jason. I'm fixing the peanut butter."

His hand trembles as he holds the glass, and he knocks his napkin and crackers off the table. "My crackers!" he wails. "My juice isn't . . . you won't . . ."

"Hurry, teacher," Edward says. "You're making him cry."

"This can won't open. Wait a moment. I think it's dented. Here, let me get another can."

"It's your fault, teacher," Alex insists. "You're making him cry."

"I'm sorry, Jason," I say, pouring his juice. "I couldn't seem to get the can open. Maybe we need a new can opener."

"And you made Jason cry, didn't you, teacher?" Lilly asks, tears of sympathy in her own eyes.

"I didn't want to make him cry," I apologize. "He must have been very thirsty."

"Or maybe his helicopter is broken," Samantha says. Something surely feels broken today to Jason, and the children recognize the feeling. "Or maybe nobody wanted to play with him."

"Maybe his mommy was shouting at him," Edward suggests.

"I think he wants me to play with him, do you?" Ira asks.

"He wants *me* to play with him," Samantha assures Ira. "He wants to be the baby. So he can stop crying, right, Jason?"

Jason finishes his juice and leaves the table. He has not responded to any offers of friendship but is in a more hopeful mood as he begins a new pile of helicopter paintings. The second one, amazingly, looks perfect to him.

"Look, teacher, this one doesn't got any mistake."

"You did it in two tries, Jason. One-two."

"Because my fingers are getting longer."

"And stronger," Petey adds.

"But not wronger," I say, laughingly, bringing out Jason's first smile of the day.

Samantha's pursuit of Jason grows more inventive. "I'm putting you in my story, Jason. Come here and listen."

"I don't want to."

"Yes, you have to. Or I won't . . . give you a piece of gum when my daddy buys some."

"Okay." Jason sits down next to Samantha and watches as she dictates her story. Had a teacher threatened him in such a manner, he would withdraw; as it is, his interest in Samantha's story is heightened. He correctly interprets her warning as a sign of friendship, and the story proves him correct.

> Once upon a time there was a little girl. Then a helicopter came. Then the little girl said hello to the helicopter. Then a kitty says hello to the helicopter. Then the kitty and the girl and the helicopter are friends.

Alex is not to be outdone. "I'm putting you in my story too, Jason. You're going to crash. In my story the helicopter crashes. Is that okay?"

"I think so," he responds, gathering a pile of papers for his helicopter pictures.

"Don't draw now, Jason," Samantha urges. "You wanna be my husband?"

"No, because I'm busy."

"Or the baby? Or the cook? Do you want to make a birthday cake? Do you want to be dead but then you come alive? Remember you liked it that time?"

As Samantha imagines other scenes, she doesn't notice that Jason has stopped drawing and instead has cut a large oval shape. "This is your cape, Samantha. To be a queen. I'm the king." But when I glance at their block castle a while later, Jason seems to be the queen's baby.

Does Samantha continue to push Jason into the baby role because he appears babyish to her? I doubt it. I have seen too many mature children prefer the baby crib in play to think there is a direct connection between outer characteristics and inner desire.

Samantha's motives, I think, are simple and understandable. She likes being the mother, and she is fond of Jason. To express her true feelings, she must act the role of his mother. The mother-baby relationship spells love most dramatically for many children. By year's end, Samantha will have moved to the big sister–little sister version of the same emotion, and Lilly will happily give up her own mother–lost child scenario to become Samantha's little sister.

It is interesting that in Samantha's helicopter story she is a little girl; perhaps it is difficult to imagine the mother's role in a helicopter fantasy. How fortunate this is for Jason, since Samantha must therefore persuade him to leave the helicopter house at least once a day. Her need to play the mother-baby scene provides Jason with the logical context for non-helicopter play. By comparison to Samantha's urgency, my plans are but empty distractions.

What about Alex's plans for Jason? He too has put him in a story, but his motives are not quite as clear as Samantha's.

"You're supposed to crash, Jason," Alex instructs him when they are together on the stage.

"I'm making my wheels go round."

"No, Jason, you got to crash to pieces. Fall down."

"It doesn't break," Jason replies.

"He means pretend," I offer to help.

"It didn't pretend," Jason argues.

"Alex, could Jason land safely? He doesn't want to crash."

"Yeah, he could. There's another helicopter crashes. Not him. Who wants to crash?" he asks, and a number of hands go up. Crashing suits most boys, but Jason is not yet willing to allow another child to have control over his crashes.

Nonetheless, the experience makes Jason bold. He jumps up as I turn to Arlene's story. "Who wants to be in this story?" he asks. "Raise your hand."

The children are puzzled for a moment, then begin to hold up their arms. Arlene herself watches with great interest.

"Who wants to be a helicopter?" Jason asks.

"I don't have a helicopter," Arlene tells him.

Jason looks at her quizzically. "What *do* you have?" Coming from Jason, the question is startling. This may be his first full acknowledgment that people create different characters, just as he has fashioned his helicopter role. His successful resistance to Alex's crashing helicopter has enabled Jason to perceive more consciously the line between "I am a helicopter" and "I *choose* to be a helicopter."

"I have a mother," Arlene says. "And she's a snake. And there's babies too."

"Are you the mother?" Jason asks. As soon as Arlene enters the stage, Jason returns to his seat. He rotates his helicopter blades slowly, whispering to himself. My guess is that he is saying, "Who wants to be the helicopter?" It is his rehearsal for the future, when he will feel comfortable in approaching another child with "Do you want to play with me? Who do you want to be?"

After school, Trish and Gail want to talk about Jason's remarkable performance.

"He was pretending to be the teacher," Gail says.

"I don't think so," Trish argues. "Uh-uh. I think he suddenly realized what these stories are all about."

"But he used Vivian's exact tone . . ."

"Yeah, I know, but I think the question itself suddenly made sense. Is there a helicopter in your story? Who wants to be the mother? These are decisions *you* make, not mysterious impositions from the outside."

"I'm a bad guy," Jason tells me. "You locked me in again."

"Who locked you in?"

"You did. Because I won't take a nap. Because I'm a helicopter. A bad helicopter."

I pretend to search for the key. "Ah, I found the key."

"Give me the key," Jason says. "Now I'm unlocking the helicopter. Someone put him in jail."

Truly it is Jason who has found the key. As he cautiously integrates new ideas into the original helicopter fantasy, I have only to watch and listen—and sometimes play the game—in order to see how the process works with him.

"Why does Jason say 'yiddle'?" asks Alex. Everyone looks at Jason, who does not seem offended.

"He can't say his *l*'s yet," I tell the children. "So 'little' sounds like 'yiddle.'"

Alex laughs when I say the word, and Jason begins to chant, "Yiddle yiddle yiddle yiddle." He wants the children to laugh at him and they do. "Yiddle yiddle yiddle," he continues as long as they keep laughing. Now they begin to copy him. "Yiddle yiddle yiddle."

"Who knows the name of this juice?" I ask, hoping to change the subject.

"Pineapple," the children shout.

"Yiddle," Jason says, and again there is laughter.

"Mr. Paley really loves pineapple juice," I state, with emphasis. The "yiddle" game makes me uncomfortable.

"Who is Mr. Paley?" Lilly asks.

"My husband."

"Our husband is daddy," she says.

"Yiddle."

"My daddy is Richard," Eli says.

"Yiddle." The children have stopped responding to Jason; they want to tell their fathers' names.

"My daddy is Big Ted," Alex says.

"Yiddle."

"Jason, what's your father's name?" I ask.

"Yiddle."

"You're lying, Jason," Alex shouts, suddenly upset. "That's not his name."

Jason whispers "Yiddle," then says "Jim."

"My baby is Jim," Lilly exclaims, delighted. "Jason, my baby is Jim and your daddy is Jim. That's funny."

"My baby is a baby too," Jason tells Lilly. "She's Sarah. She spits up."

"Guess what? So does my baby. Both our babies is the same."

I am relieved to see the end of the "yiddle" game. Yet it points to an important change in Jason: He wants the children to laugh at him, which is to say, he wants them to like him.

When he entered school, fear set aside this ordinary desire. You can make connections with a few people, but unless you want everyone to like you, the bonds are shaky and undependable.

Much of what I do that is good in the classroom is motivated, I am sure, by my desire to be liked by the children and by my assistants. I do not wish to deny this fact, because it exerts a strong pull among us all. Unless we want to be liked by others, the classroom culture does not yield its magic.

Staying a moment longer with my own case, what specific acts of mine are intended, no matter what other accompanying benefits, to cause my classroom family to like me? Everything that demonstrates my interest and affection. I listen carefully to people's ideas; I quote them to one another; I laugh at their jokes (though I didn't laugh at "yiddle," I admit) and try sometimes to make them laugh at me; I tell good stories and respond gratefully to the ones I hear.

All of the above are certainly elements in a plan to encourage growth and change in others, but in addition I am promoting my own cause. In my secret fantasy, the children tell their families, "I *like* Mrs. Paley. She's the nicest teacher."

When I was a new teacher, it was the principal's approval I sought. I was afraid of the children. There were too many of them always surrounding me, people I was supposed to influence and cause to improve in all ways, quickly and visibly, so that my principal would like me.

Only as I began to seek the children's approval could I concentrate on individual needs and differences. If you want a certain person to like you, then you find out what makes him or her happy. I began to realize that I could not teach much to anyone unless the person liked me a lot.

Jason's "yiddle" game is a sign that he wants us to like him, but why has he waited so long? During the first months of school, Simon and Joseph tried, in every way they could think of, to entice him into their play, but he refused. He was too fearful to care if the boys liked him—as was I in my early teaching years. There were too many people in this classroom that needed to be influenced; Jason could think only of self-preservation and control.

Jason's most reliable tool has been the helicopter; mine had been drills and exercises. Both Jason and I, as newcomers to a classroom, hovered over children without landing on their runways, without entering their fantasies.

I cannot avoid my own premises and experiences, and I can only pretend to know Jason's. But he is a child who causes me to analyze myself and everyone else. In his visible confusion, he often clarifies matters for me.

For example, my routine question, "Is there a helicopter in the story?" intended to help Jason think about the effect of a helicopter flying into a story-in-progress, did not lessen Jason's bewilderment. He may have heard the question simply as a signal to cease his activity, without further meaning.

Come to think of it, my question *is* misleading. Since I have the printed story before me, I must already know if it contains a helicopter. A more honest response from me would be: "There's no helicopter in this story, Jason. You must raise your hand if you want to be one of the characters in Simon's story."

When the children began to put helicopters in their stories, he was then able to ask himself his own urgent questions: Will the author have power over me? Will I surrender a piece of me if I act in this story?

Not all children respond with such intensity. For Katie, issues of power and influence seem to create few obstacles. This is a fortunate characteristic, but we are wrong to heap credit on her simply because she has fewer problems of this sort to overcome than do other children.

Katie draws pictures frequently for her classmates and provides us with splendid examples of gift giving and "niceness," the very thing people do when they want to be liked. Yet, on the two occasions when Jason gave a gift—a helicopter picture for Arlene's story and a queen's cape for Samantha—the angels must have sung. Did Jason make these gifts because he wanted to be liked? I think, knowing Jason, he was curious to know how he would feel.

Wanting to be liked is a major commitment, with far-reaching positive implications for school life. It is well to ask ourselves, before denying a child certain kinds of behaviors, if the child is trying to find a way to be liked. Is the behavior designed to make us laugh?

Laughter is not enough for Jason; he seeks other connections. "Do you have a helicopter?" he asks Alex.

"No."

He repeats the question, moments later. "Alex, do you have a helicopter?"

"No."

When Jason asks a third time, I say, "Did you want Alex to play helicopter with you?"

"My blades are broken. I have to fix them."

As I resume my place at the story table, I hear, "Alex, do

you have a helicopter?" What is Jason's question about, I wonder.

Alex doesn't seem puzzled. "I might get one."

"This kind?"

"Yeah, I think so."

When Joseph arrives, Jason begins to question him in the same way. "What kind of helicopter do you have, Joseph?"

"I don't have one anymore."

"Do you have a helicopter?"

Joseph stares at Jason. "I didn't get a helicopter."

"Do you have this kind?"

"No."

Why does Jason continue in this manner? Perhaps he can now imagine himself playing helicopter with another child but cannot imagine someone holding one of his helicopters. Even within the safety of a story, his helicopter is not to be touched. This must be a great struggle for Jason. He wants to play as others do and has made important beginnings, but at the heart of his play is the helicopter, *his* helicopter, that glorious, private symbol he cannot share. Does Jason suspect, I wonder, that an even more glorious feeling awaits him, the freedom to share his fantasy with another child.

"Why not just buy a fleet of helicopters for the classroom?" Trish suggests, pouring out her coffee. We haven't finished cleaning up, but she is eager to talk about Jason's helicopter questions, so we bring our thermoses to a clean table.

"But, Trish, if we do that, aren't we side-stepping the issue?" Gail asks. "By the way, Vivian, how is it we don't have a helicopter or two?"

"We had several last year and they all got broken. But there are two little planes in the box, and no one plays with them. What issue would we be side-stepping?"

"Well, wouldn't this be a case of stepping in with the solution before we know the problem?"

"Right," Trish agrees. "Look what happened in music. Why

did Jason have to leave the group when they all pretended to be helicopters?"

"That surprised me too," I say. "He seemed overwhelmed. And I was so sure my helicopter song would make him happy. You know, most of my ideas don't work with Jason. He either takes his clues from the children or figures things out for himself."

"Why don't we just wait and see what Jason does on his own," Trish proposes. "He must have his own reasons for asking people if they have helicopters—and it is his question, not ours."

"Something really bothers me," Gail says suddenly. "Why can't Jason just *keep* the helicopter fantasy to himself? Does it matter, really?"

"I think it does," I respond quickly. "Because it's possible that Jason misunderstands the fantasy-reality issue and that his helicopter play is merely the way he reveals the confusion. I mean, what if Jason is afraid to allow someone into his fantasy for the same reason he worries about playing along with another child's fantasy? Once you get in, you can't get out."

"And the other child might gain control over him?"

"Or frighten him and he wouldn't be able to fly back to a safe place."

"Or even take away his helicopter." Trish and Gail spill over with possibilities. "It's sort of mystical, isn't it?" Gail asks.

"Sure. Children *are* mystical. Let's keep watching Jason and see if we can pinpoint some of these misunderstandings. For instance, yesterday he made a squirrel hole out of the crates upstairs. Whenever Simon approached, Jason pretended it was a helicopter house, but if anyone else came near, he called it a squirrel hole. Why? Well, the squirrel hole image is *Simon's*. Isn't Jason revealing a fear of taking another child's fantasy?"

"Like stealing his shadow—or his soul?" Trish ponders her own idea for a while, then blurts out, "But this is impossible! Will I have to analyze twenty-four or more children this way when I have my own class? I'll have no time for anything else!"

"But Trish, the teacher doesn't do all the work," I remind

her, and she winks at Gail. I am about to embark upon one of my favorite subjects. "The children correct one another's misconceptions all the time while they play and work and talk and act in each other's stories. It's only when a classroom is set up to isolate children that the teacher is required to make all the connections—obviously, an impossible task."

The next morning I do seem to capture a moment of truth when I realize that Jason doesn't know—*really* know—the relationship between the stories we dictate and those we act out in the story room.

In the middle of Samantha's story, Jason says to me, "I'm in my story being a helicopter and someone else is going to be a helicopter . . ." He doesn't attempt to enter Samantha's story; he speaks as if he has just sat down at the story table to dictate his own story.

"But, Jason, look," I say, pointing to the stage. "We're in the middle of Samantha's story."

"Where's mine?"

"You didn't do one today."

"I did! I'm a helicopter in it! I did it!"

"Don't worry, Jason. You *thought* it, in your head. Probably you were too busy to tell me."

"I'm telling you all the time!" he complains. "And you always tell me not to."

"I'll remind you tomorrow, Jason. I promise."

Once again, Jason demonstrates the exact point at which he is blocked. Others, similarly troubled, keep going *as if* they understand, waiting for time and experience to sort out each new layer of doubt. But Jason wants to clear up "mistakes" before moving ahead.

Merely saying to Jason, "Tell me your story and I'll write it down so we can act it out" doesn't inform either one of us of what he knows about the process. Or of how long it will take him to learn. Children do not appear with printed calendars, as on packets of seeds, to advise us when a given concept will germinate for them and then burst into flower.

If I am eager to discover how Jason clarifies his view of storytelling, I must patiently watch and listen. My guess is that the insights he requires will emerge indirectly and not while he is dictating a story. But no one can tell where the moments of truth lie for another person—or even for oneself.

"It's time to go to bed, dad," Lilly tells Eli.

"First don't we watch TV a little bit in the night?"

"And then it wakes the baby? Yeah, let's do that!"

How odd that this is considered an exciting plot. No adult would suggest these events as the focus of a good piece of theater.

"But we need a kid that wakes up. Edward . . .?" Edward is telephoning. "I'm the police. You have to call me. Get Jason. He's just painting."

"Jason, Jason, come here!"

Uncharacteristically, Jason answers the call, perhaps because Lilly is speaking. "What do you want?"

"We need a kid, Jason," Eli says. "Or a doll?"

"No doll," Lilly decides. "We need a real baby. Or you could be a kid. Okay, Jason?" She gently lowers a bib over Jason's head, and he doesn't object. "There. Lie down, small child. And I have to put a pretty dress on and then the dad and mom watch TV and then the baby cries because we waked you up."

Lilly and Eli push two chairs together and stare at a picture on the wall. Suddenly, Eli jumps up and turns an imaginary knob. "It's loud now, mom. Cry, Jason. It waked you up."

"Wah wah wah."

"Sorry, baby, we'll make it soft. Goodnight. Go back to sleep."

Jason closes his eyes and, in a few minutes, the drama is repeated. "Wah wah wah." Jason performs his role perfectly. It is immensely satisfying for him and the others as they retrace each step: sit down, watch TV, turn it louder, make the baby cry, apologize, turn it down, begin again.

After four or five repetitions, it is time for an extension of the plot. "Did you call the police?" Edward asks. "I'm on the phone for you to call me."

Lilly immediately dials the other telephone. "Police, police, someone's waking the baby!"

"Who is it?"

"Maybe a robber. We saw him on TV."

"Okay. Call me again if he wakes up the baby."

Now a new routine begins: watch TV, point to the robber on the TV set, call the police to report that the robber is waking the baby, return to the TV set. Here is a clearly organized lesson in group fantasy play for Jason to study. The characters are named; the sequence of events is described in advance and precisely followed; the pattern is repeated.

Such must be the way Jason will learn to fit his helicopter into society, through rhythmic little echo-plays that are not too dissimilar from the game of broken blades and fixed blades that he invented for himself. True, Simon and Joseph have been suggesting ideas all along, but apparently Jason lacked the practice in this art form to adapt their wider-ranging variations to his own play.

The doll corner is a good place for the novice, with its soothing, repetitive domestic routines, but Jason prefers the more private vantage point of his helicopter house, just as Simon once needed his squirrel hole.

"This hole is caving in," Simon calls out.

"I'll call the police," Jason responds, to Simon's surprise.

"Helicopter police?"

Jason pretends to dial. "Helicopter police, helicopter police, answer the phone six, seven, eight."

"Tell them I'm caving in."

"He's caving in."

"Never mind. I dug myself out. Oh oh oh this hole is caving in again! Oh oh oh help!"

"Helicopter police, helicopter police, answer the phone. He's caving in." Jason dials rapidly.

"Never mind. I dug myself out."

I want to cheer and shout, "You've got it! You've really got it!" The helicopter has heard a cry of distress and called for help. No matter how deep the hole or high the wall, the voices of other children will penetrate. The children's manipulation of one another's play provokes a genuine self-awareness that the adult cannot emulate. Now that Jason is on his way, there is so much to learn.

Alex is in a teasing mood. "That don't even look like a helicopter, Jason."

Jason collects his breath for a scream, then changes his mind. "It *is* a helicopter!"

"Then why aren't you in the sky ha ha?"

"This is where I sit," Jason replies, perplexed.

"You're not in the sky nya nya."

"But I'm . . . when I . . . in the sky . . ."

"Nya nya my gummy bear plane I'm in can fly better than you."

Surprisingly, Jason laughs. "This is a stupid helicopter. A stupid stupid nothing," he says, trying to ingratiate himself as he did with "yiddle."

Alex accepts Jason's good-natured response and offers one of his own. "Hey Jason, you're flying way up there! Wow! You're really high up. Samantha, look at Jason up in the sky."

"Meow meow," Samantha licks her paws. "Meow meow I'm a kitty now meow meow."

"It's a kitty airport," Jason says eagerly. "Yeah, a kitty airport. For kitties. Samantha, where's kitty?"

Samantha is momentarily puzzled. This is a new Jason; she is not entirely sure how to react. Then she trusts her instincts. "Meow meow, here's your kitty."

"Where's kitty?" Jason repeats. "Here kitty, here kitty." He removes two blocks to create a door for Samantha. "Here kitty, where's kitty?" he calls.

"Meow meow, here's your kitty," Samantha purrs. She crawls between and around the blocks of the heliport as Jason strokes her hair. This is as good a doll corner scene as anyone has devised, and Jason needs no one's advice on how to extend the plot.

"Meow meow meow."

Jason bends down to whisper, "Okay, the lady isn't going to lock you out. If you get out, I'll put you back in. Here kitty meow meow.

"Oh oh, the lady locked you out. Here's kitty. I'll put you back in. Here kitty meow meow."

Later, when Jason sits beside me to tell his story, I cannot resist saying, "I wonder if you'll have a kitty in your story."

"No," he responds, surprised.

"I heard you and Samantha playing kitty before."

"No." He does not intend to discuss his experience or put it into a story. "There goes the helicopter," he begins. "Up up up in the sky. And the blades are so fast. That helicopter is so fast. And it will never land. The end."

At going home time, Jason pulls his jacket off the hook and tells me, "There's a baby in my tummy."

"Like mommy had?"

"The baby has a cubby inside. The lady lets her out."

We cannot uncover every thought that influences a child. Nor is it necessary. The connections between one event and another will be made in the process of living, at home and at school. In both places the adult who listens and responds to what the children say can be an important guide. But the children themselves will unlock—or lock, if need be—the doors to their secrets as they play out their scenes; and the images in their minds will be adapted to the people and events around them.

"Who's my friend?" Jason asks me.

"Is it Samantha?"

"She's my kitty friend."

"The mother kitty?"

"She can't. Because I let *her* in, she doesn't let me in."

"Are you the big kitty?"

"No, I'm a big person. I'm eight."

"So what, Jason," Alex interjects. "My brother is *nine.*"

"So what, *my* brother is ten," Jason replies. He doesn't have a brother, but he's learning how to play an important game.

"What would we talk about without Jason?" Gail asks me when I report the latest conversation.

"Now, wait. I'll bet if we kept a record, we'd find that we speak just as often about Samantha and Alex and Simon and the others."

"Well, if we do," Trish laughs, "it's mainly because you're always proving to us that they do the same things Jason does, only in different ways."

"By the way, speaking of Samantha," Trish says, "why does she like Jason so much? There are others who will gladly be her baby. Why Jason?"

"Yeah, I wonder about that, too," Gail nods. "She's almost five and a leader, certainly, of the big girls. Why Jason?"

"Why meow meow meow?"

"Why wha-wha-wha?"

"Why gr-r-r-ow?"

"Why br-r-r-ah?"

The three of us burst out laughing, and Trish begins to dance around the table. In response, Gail winds up her arms and helicopters through the room while I drop to my knees meowing. My colleagues converge upon me and begin rubbing my neck, murmuring, "Where's kitty, here's kitty, nice kitty."

"Whew! That felt good," Gail sighs, stretching out on the floor. "So that's why they keep it up all morning."

"I'll bet we can't understand the half of it," I say, sitting up suddenly. "Hey, you know what? Most children start school with 'Here kitty meow meow' and then gradually expose their discontents. Jason does it the other way. It's taken him months to work up to 'Here kitty meow meow.' First, as he's told us many times, he needed to make his mistakes."

"You're going to laugh at me," Trish says. "I'm the same way. Really. I've spent six months doing everything wrong. But lately I'm feeling a little bit 'Here kitty meow meow.'"

"Ah, how nice," I say. "Me too, only make that *years*, not months. Believe me, I've had my own helicopter houses."

"Like what?"

"Well, Jason's helicopter house has kept him insulated from the fantasies of others, and the drills and tests served that purpose for me, in the early years."

"What do you think happened to the children's fantasies when you were like that?"

"I think they were always there, waiting to be activated. I just didn't take advantage of them. The children played them out and I wasn't listening. Their main subject never became part of the school curriculum."

These days I'm feeling ambivalent about fairy tales for young children. Even when I use my own words and modify the danger potential, the children seem worried. Samantha and Lilly take turns asking if someone is about to be eaten or lost, and Arlene wants to know if I'm telling it "the real way." Real means scary.

Even so, the discussions afterward tend to be quite remarkable. By the time most children are four they can identify and debate many of the issues hidden in these age-old plots. Today, even Jason is moved to join a discussion of "The Three Pigs."

"I wonder if the mother pig missed her children," I ask, thinking immediately that this is too manipulative a question.

"She's not nice," Lilly responds. "She made them go away from her."

"Because she couldn't handle them, Lilly," Samantha says.

"Yeah, she lost all her money," Joseph adds.

"Maybe a thief came and took it," Alex says.

"But Lilly is sorry she made her children leave." And I'm sorry I asked a question that makes Lilly feel sad. "Probably she didn't know there was a wolf," I say.

"She did know!" Joseph argues. "See, she wanted the boys

to get away before the wolf came so she could trick him and she could stick him with a stick."

"She could stick a fork through the wolf," Vinnie says.

"She could shoot a gun. I'll do it right now. Pk-k-k." Jason aims his helicopter blade at the center of the rug.

"They didn't have guns in those houses, Jason. She has to use a axe."

"Or a fire, Simon," Jason replies. "And boiling water."

"Your idea is interesting, Joseph. You think she had a feeling there might be a wolf coming so she thought of this idea to save her boys. She sent them away."

"And the children wouldn't be home," he says. "And she was stronger."

"Stronger than the wolf?" I ask.

Everyone nods in agreement. "Much stronger. The mother is much much stronger," they tell one another.

I have another question up my sleeve. "I wonder if the pigs ever go back to live with their mother." There is an immediate chorus of yesses.

"She misses her children," Edward says.

"Because she doesn't like it to be alone with the baby," Jason decides.

"Oh, do you think she had a baby at home?"

The children ponder the notion in silence. It is an awesome moment. "Naw, she didn't, Jason," Joseph responds. "She was too poor."

"And she was too busy," Alex adds. The children don't want to think of a baby at home while the little pigs are out in the forest with the wolf.

"But Jason thinks there might be a baby," I remind them.

"Jason, see, that baby is the littlest pig," Katie explains. "That pig went away too."

"I think maybe they could go back to live in their old house and they would see the wolf hanged up on the wall," Joseph states with finality, as if he can envision the entire inside of the mother's house.

"Where is the daddy?" I wonder.

"They don't have a daddy."

"Maybe he got killed by the wolf," Alex suggests.

"He did, he did! He was out hunting and the wolf killed him."

"No," Jason says. "He's at work."

"Yeah, he's flying in a plane to a meeting."

"He might be in a hotel visiting some place."

"And when he comed back," Alex decides, "the mother told him don't worry the children will be home in a minute."

"How shall we act this out?" I ask. "The way I told it the pigs don't get eaten by the wolf."

"That's not the real way," Simon says.

"I don't like the real way," Lilly replies, and everyone agrees with her, including Simon.

"Okay, the pigs run to their brother's brick house. Now how about the ending? I had the wolf run off to another forest but, in most books, he's cooked in boiling water."

"In the chimney," Jason completes the image. This is the most involved he has ever become in a formal group discussion.

"Yeah, he's boiled!" They all seem to agree.

"All right. Who will be the wolf?" I ask.

There are no volunteers. Had the wolf been in a child's story, several hands would be raised. But there is a wariness about taking this role in an adult-conceived tale.

"Well, we do need a wolf."

"I'll be the wolf if he runs away," Alex offers.

"Shall we let the wolf run away then?" I ask. There are no objections, and we begin.

The children have gained control of "The Three Pigs" through discussion and dramatics, and the effect is not lost on Jason. The next morning he wants to know if Arlene has a wolf in her story.

"Is there a big bad wolf in there?" he asks her.

"There might be," she replies.

Once upon a time came a mommy and a daddy.

Then came a brother and a little girl. The mommy
had a sword. Then the daddy said, "Why do you
have a sword?" "Because there's a wolf in my story."
Then they go to sleep.

Arlene has been watching Jason. "You want to be the wolf,
Jason?"

"Does he get boiled?"

"He runned away when he seed the sword."

"Okay," Jason agrees, but once in the story room, he changes
his mind. Then, as each story is taken from the pile to be read
and acted, he asks the author if there is a wolf in the story.

Jason is not a slow learner; he is a cautious researcher. He
takes each new idea and collects data on its application until
he is satisfied that he knows every response and reaction it
might receive in the outside world. He expects mistakes and
wants them to occur in his own controlled setting.

There are a number of ideas Jason is at work on right now.
He has expanded his break-and-fix theme to include a lost and
found kitty, a locked and unlocked house, and an occasional
squirrel or baby. In his many repetitions he examines the ways
in which the players control the fantasy and allow themselves
to change roles and move back and forth between several points
of view. In this, Samantha is a constant goad and agent of
reform.

"This is my two-seater," Jason tells Samantha.

"Let me be the mother driver."

"You can't. You're the little kitty."

"No I'm not. I'm the mother dog. You're my baby doggy,
Jason."

"Look at the fan belt. It's broken. I have to fix it."

"Jason! No! We're doggies. Just be a doggy! Then I'll look at
the fan belt later. Come on, you won't be a really doggy baby,
just only pretend. Jason, listen, stop turning that! You're really
a helicopter really but you're *pretending* a baby, okay, Jason,
okay?"

Jason has been staring at Samantha during her outburst, thumb in his mouth and his eyes growing larger.

"Well, well?" Samantha is annoyed with her friend. "Come on, Jason, or I won't play with you *ever.* Then later I'll look at the fan belt *ten times.*"

Jason laughs and replies, "Woof-woof."

"Good. Here's your bottle, little doggy. Put your foot like that. Pretend you can't walk yet and I have to teach you. Come on, little doggy, your mother is taking you to doggy school so you can get big."

Samantha's explanation, "You're really a helicopter really but you're pretending a baby" could never be used by a teacher. The statement can only be made by another child, because it must stay within the child's context of reality. Coming from a child it means, "You're really *pretending* to be a helicopter but, for a moment, the helicopter will pretend to be a baby."

If I told Jason he was really a helicopter he would become confused; he depends on the adult to know he is a boy. Yet, once, when I said to him, "I know you're pretending to be a helicopter," he cried in anger, "I *am* a helicopter!" The adult's and child's points of view cannot meet sensibly on this issue. When Samantha tells Jason he is a pretend or real *anything*, he knows she accepts his persona on the same basis as he himself does, without altering his internal or external position.

In this single exchange between two young children there are important implications for classroom teaching at all levels. Children are able to teach one another best if they are permitted to interact socially and playfully throughout the day.

Samantha zealously shows Jason how to move between two positions, which is to say, to study another point of view. When they are older, they will teach each other how to alter other perspectives: from past tense to present, from one mathematical system to another, from one subject to another. Where attitudes and perceptions must be changed, teacher and learner do well to begin with similar premises.

Of course, premise is not all there is to know about the learner. There is *style*—an often overlooked factor. Jason, for example, seems to need many samples of a single point, whereas Joseph wants to see everything at once—and then fill in the holes when no one is watching.

Come to think of it, Jason reminds me of Fritz, my graduate school friend of long ago who went from classroom to classroom checking out a single question for his dissertation: What is the relationship between a teacher's perception of a troublesome child and the reality of the case? Day after day, Fritz watched both Charles and my reaction to Charles until he had seen us under every sort of circumstance.

Jason works the same way, though he is not an impartial observer. He flew his helicopter into the children's stories and noted their consistently negative responses. Meanwhile, certain of his ideas, repeated often, have become familiar games.

The "Simon is outside the window" research is a perfect example of the latter. "I see Simon outside the window," Jason still says about once a week, but Simon's initial anger has turned to amusement.

"Yeah, I'm sitting on a tree."

"I see Simon outside in a tree."

"Yeah, I'm flying in the sky."

"I see Simon in the sky."

"Yeah, I'm on the moon. I'm a moon guy."

"Moon boom."

Simon thinks it's funny so Jason continues to see a squirrel outside the window; the children become angry so Jason no longer flies into stories. Unlike Fritz, who announced his goals before beginning a research project, Jason recognizes a goal after the fact. His "Do you have a helicopter?" is not so simple a question as Fritz's "Who do you think is the worst child in your class?"

Both questions, however, are sincere attempts to study the classroom, and both questioners demonstrate the excitement of chasing after that which they don't know. Fritz couldn't wait to tell me every day what he was discovering in my classroom, and Jason is beginning to do the same thing.

"Look, teacher! I told Simon he's outside the window and he flied to the moon."

"Every time you tell him he's outside he makes up a new story."

"I see Simon outside in a tree!" Jason says gleefully.

"You can't see me, Jason, because my squirrely hole is invisible." The boys think Simon's newest response is hilarious, but no more so than Fritz and I did about some of Charles's inventions. Both Fritz and Jason have made me see the classroom in more human terms, and there are few behaviors more human than laughter and invention.

"Look at this thing." Jason shows me a construction made of small plastic squares. "Look at, teacher. I builded this. If you get down. It's sort of a plane it goes up here and then look how far. Then I have to make it again."

"You like it better when you build your own plane, I think. Better than a plane from a store."

"Why do I?"

"Then you can take it apart and build it again."

"I really do take it apart."

"Not pretend. You really do take it apart."

Pretend is one of the subjects Jason is studying. It is not easy. Here he is really taking apart something that is a pretend airplane but which he calls a real airplane. At noon, waiting to be picked up, Jason demonstrates the dimensions of his problems with pretend. As we arrange ourselves on the front steps, Alex accidentally sits on Jason's feet, and Jason responds, "Oh! He's pretending to sit on my feet."

Alex is surprised. "No I didn't pretend. I really did sit on your feet."

"You really did?"

"But it was a accident."

"Oh."

Jason uses pretend in an unfamiliar way, surprising even another child. Is it a simple error, a slip of the tongue, or does this represent a deep confusion?

What if Jason thinks pretending something makes it accidentally happen? These are concepts that cannot be taught, but scenes such as the following, played out a few feet from his heliport, should provide a broad area in which to study the enigma.

"Pretend you're the baby brother plane," Simon says. "And I'm the daddy. Tell me you're scared."

"I'm scared, daddy," Joseph replies.

"Don't worry, baby brother plane, you won't fall out. I'm locking up two doors. Look at the door. It's a exit door. You can't fall out. Fly up higher."

Joseph is, apparently, at the same time, the baby brother plane *and* the baby brother on the plane. Locking the door keeps the baby brother and the plane itself from falling out. It is complicated for me but not for Joseph and Simon, whose play is often worked out on several levels.

Yet, if Jason is the sort of child who measures each new experience with a teaspoon, he could be blocked by the very richness of the play that surrounds him. His own play—the part we hear—is monochromatic by comparison. If there is a baby sister helicopter in his mind, the effort required to keep the unwanted image at bay might prevent Jason from opening the doors to his play.

Once he gives himself over to full-scale fantasy play with others, anything hidden may emerge. If pretend induces the accidental, how can one predict what will happen? Did Alex really not see Jason's feet? Was he pretending in his mind to sit on Jason's feet, and therefore it occurred?

In a way, pretend *does* cause accidents. We have all experienced, during a moment of fantasy, the appearance of a long forgotten and unwelcome memory. This must be happening to

Jason, and he is cautious; he has good reason to believe that, in spontaneous play, such "accidents" are more likely to materialize.

Lest I appear to make too much of a singular incident, it is no more, I think, than Jason himself does. He takes errors seriously. He wraps himself in one fantasy, learns all its pitfalls, and avoids any extracurricular fantasy in which mistakes or accidents might occur. He practices mistakes, perhaps in order to recognize one quickly when it comes along. I call my analytical exercises *teaching:* Jason calls his *play.*

As my imagination leads me from one rationalization to another, the children follow their instincts into dramatic interpretations of the same events. Their group fantasy is a round table discussion in story form.

"The drawbridge is opening!" Simon shouts.

"Hurry it up! The airport is closing," Joseph responds.

"Pretend it can't open. Hey, Jason, make a drawbridge like we got and then we pretend ours is stuck and we fly around and then we see yours, okay?"

"I don't got a drawbridge."

"Then you can't keep out bad guys ha-ha!"

"Ha-ha yourself!" Samantha retorts. "Jason doesn't have bad guys."

"But sometimes I'm one, Samantha," he tells her.

"Oh, when the teacher locked you up in there?"

"Yeah, and then Joseph found the key," Jason remembers with satisfaction. "And sometimes I make bad crashes."

"And then you fix it, right?"

It is pointless for me to protest that I did not in fact lock anyone up, for they are using the incident in order to discuss good and bad. Jason and his helicopter are both good and bad, creating scenes that help bail them out of trouble and despair.

And who am I while all this is going on? Well, when I jump into someone's fantasy and insist it is all wrong, I must be the bad wolf or the witch.

"Boys, boys! Look what you're doing!" The doll corner is a

blizzard of dress-ups and pillows. "And we just cleaned up. Now hang all those things up, *please!*"

"We smothered the robbers," Joseph says.

"But you left a huge mess for the teachers." From the looks on their faces, my disapproval may be worse than the time-out chair.

There is a whispered conference, a moment of silence, and then, when I am presumably out of range of hearing, Simon says, "Look in the bathroom there. A blue witch with gray hair."

"A gray monster! She can make a fire in her mouth!"

"Watch her! She's looking."

Pretending I've not heard, I call out, "Boys, I could use your help here, if you have the time. I splattered paint on the sinks. Tell you what. I'll help you in there, then you can help me with the brushes and sink in here."

Simon hugs me when I come in and, seeing me return the hug, Joseph and Edward rush to throw their arms around me. As I've said before, there's nothing quite so grand a feeling as helping one another out of a trap.

But some traps are harder to climb out of than others. "You're blocking both doorways, Jason," I call out later from the story table. "No one will be able to go into the hallway." Our classroom, created out of several bedrooms of an old house, has two doors, side by side. "We have a rule, Jason. Nobody can cover both doors at once."

"Don't say that to me!" Jason cries angrily.

"I must tell you the rule, Jason."

He continues to pile up blocks across both entrances. "Don't come back and say it."

"Jason, you may not cover both doors. Decide which doorway you like best. I'll help you move the other blocks."

"No, no!" He is now crying furiously. "Pushing blocks! I'm going to be pushing blocks!"

"Don't push them down. You'll hurt someone."

"It would be horrible," he screams. "Horrible horrible horrible if I knock down the building."

"Don't do it, please."

Jason stands still, crying softly. "I'm going to stop crying. I'm going to open one door all the way open. I'm not going to push the blocks." He says all these things in a stilted manner, as if speaking firmly to himself.

I put my arm around him. "Thanks, Jason. That's a big help."

Jason turns to me, wiping his eyes. "If you walk through this way, all the school building will fall down."

"Pretend fall down?"

"Pretend school building," he replies.

Jason speaks to his tiny Lego people and makes each figure push down a plastic tree. "Don't, don't do that! Look, teacher, they push down all the trees. I told them only push down seven. Aren't they bad?"

Some might insist that Jason is simply demonstrating very young behavior, the two-year-old's acting out of parental no-no's. "Immature" is the most familiar negative label throughout the school years.

For me, such labels are useless. A child is always at a certain complex point of development; like Jason, everyone, in every endeavor, will continue to use techniques from the past in order to understand and work out ways to live securely in the present.

Once changes begin, they happen fast. The child leaps and expands in several directions, according to a mysterious plan that no one can anticipate. During one week in April, Jason is a "she-baby airplane" on Monday, a "smaller person" looking for Easter eggs on Tuesday, a "morning and night boy" on Wednesday, an angry "fighting person" on Thursday, and, on Friday, he finds a remarkable new role for his helicopter that takes my breath away in admiration and wonder.

Monday

Jason puts a she-baby and a monster in his story:

> This airplane is spinning. This airplane is stopping.
> Now this nose doesn't come up it just the wheels go
> down.

So far the story sounds the same as his others. He reaches
for a pile of papers and, thinking he is done, I tell Lilly it is
her turn to tell a story.

"I'm not finished," Jason says.

> There's a she-baby airplane that is not spinning. The
> end. *Not* the end. And a monster. The end.

Jason is the she-baby airplane when we act out his story. He
lies face down on the rug, arms straight out, not spinning.
Simon, as the airplane, roars around the room and Lilly, the
monster, gives a quiet growl. Before the story is over, one
thumb of the she-baby's wing rests securely in its mouth.

Tuesday

"This is your bed, Samantha. I made you a bed and now I'm
making my own bed."

"Yours is too short, Jason. Make it longer like mine."

"I'm pretending to be a smaller person."

"You growed bigger, Jason. Look, you need a long bed now."

"No, I'm a smaller person and in the morning I'll look all
over the house for the Easter eggs."

Samantha likes Jason's idea. "It *is* Easter the next day'and
the bunny will give you a egg when the night is finished."

Wednesday

We are upstairs in the climbing room when Jason has his
biggest tantrum of the year. He is at the top of the A-frame
ladder and does not want anyone else to climb on it. He
screams at Vinnie to get off.

"She doesn't have to, Jason. It's large enough for several children."

"Don't say that to me! Push her off, push *me* off!" He throws himself on the pad and begins to bang his head.

"Stop Jason. You mustn't do that. You're going to hurt yourself."

"Sarah does it. The babysitter lets her do it."

"I won't allow you to do it. And stop screaming. Look at Vinnie. You're scaring her."

Jason is frantic. "My teacher won't let me . . ." He stops suddenly. From the other room he hears "Nighttime–morning time, nighttime–morning time." Just those words, but they astonish him. He raises himself from the pad and stands at the doorway.

"Nighttime," Eli calls.

"Morning time," Lilly responds.

"No, we didn't get a chance to sleep. It's night for a while longer."

"The morning is coming. It's coming. Morning! It came out!" Everyone jumps up and runs around until someone shouts "Nighttime" again.

"I'm a morning-night boy too," Jason announces, and he lies down on two overturned milk crates as the others are doing.

"Still nighttime. Still nighttime."

"Morning is coming. It's coming, coming, coming, it's out!"

Jason actually looks different. His worried frown has been replaced by calm pleasure. There is something in this night-time–morning time game that has explained away his terrors and secured a vision of blissful dawn.

Thursday

"I'm having a fight with everyone with all these people," Jason calls out as he enters the block area. He swings his arms around and nearly topples Ira's building.

"Stop Jason. Fight somewhere else," Ira says.

"I want to fight!"

"Meow meow meow," Samantha purrs, ready for some kitty play.

"I'm fighting, Samantha."

"Not here, Jason!" Joseph snaps. "Go fight on the moon."

"I'm angry and I'm fighting!" This time he pushes one of Ira's blocks down.

"Teacher, teacher, look what he's doing!"

"I'm a fighting person," Jason cries, his face wet with tears. "I'm *pretending* I'm angry!"

"Oh, pretending," I say, smoothing his hair. "Let me put a cool cloth on your face. It feels hot."

"I'm not sick!"

"I know. But pretending to be angry can make someone feel hot. Come on, I'll make you cool and dry." Jason's hand is limp in mine.

"First cool, then dry," I murmur.

"Cool and dry," he echoes.

We play our own mother-child game in the bathroom. This too is part of teaching. When Jason is calm we rock for a while on the big chair and I sing one of the moon songs I remember from my summer camp days. Afterward, Jason says he wants to tell a story.

> The Easter bunny comes and brings a twisting airplane. That's what I sometimes call a helicopter. A twisting airplane. And the Easter bunny comes to a girl's house and leaves a twisting airplane for the girl. And the girl wakes up in the morning time after the nighttime and she sees the twisting airplane. And Samantha is the girl. And I'm the Easter bunny and I'm also the twisting airplane. The end.

Friday

"Do you want to play, Jason?" Samantha asks.

"Yes. You sit there. I made a two-seater. Wait, a three-seater. One more seat it needs."

"Why?"

"Because I'm going to pick someone up at school. Because not anyone will come to pick them up and walk them home. They're going to hold everyone's hand. One kid's going to hold the other kid's hand."

"And I'm the mom, okay?"

"Yes, and everyone when I get out of school I'm coming to pick them up in my airplane. No one, don't, wait, you sit down on the porch. The propeller will stop. This is the front and this is the tail."

"Do I get in now?" Samantha asks.

"Now get in. Pretend you're holding a kid's hand. Now I'm flying you to your house so you're not walking home."

"I'll be the kid, Jason, okay?" Simon asks from the squirrel hole.

"Yes, you're the kid. Hold your mom's hand. I'm flying you home."

Half a dozen times, in the past few months, I've said to myself: Now, right now, school is really beginning for Jason. Yet, this scene I have just witnessed must surely be the beginning—or is it the culmination?

Jason, finally, has figured out his own way to use his most precious possession and private fantasy to enable him to play with others. He has, in a real sense, come home. Which is to say, school is starting to feel like home. He can breathe deeply and open the doors of his helicopter house to others.

Yet, this notion of a breakthrough is mine, not Jason's. These "moments of truth" dramatize and illuminate my own fantasy play as a teacher, helping me to focus on a single child within the group.

The children do the same in play, announcing their breakthroughs as new ideas in a story. But storytellers do not keep going in the same direction; sometimes they pull back in order to examine a particular point or retrace an old theme.

"Pretend you're the pokey little puppy, Jason."

"I can't, Samantha. My two-seater is broken. Now I see only one seat. It's going to be a three-seater when I fix it."

"Aren't you playing with me?"

"No. I have to fix this helicopter seat. This three-seater."

This is Jason's way of learning, a cautious way, and it must not be misconstrued as *not* learning. The stories have helped him learn to tolerate moments of doubt because the sources of control are clearly illustrated: author, teacher, paper, stage, and a dependable format governing the performance of each participant. Surprises are there, but they are academic in style. It is an intellectual activity of the highest order and well suited to Jason, the circumspect researcher who follows the effects of one event at a time.

In play, Jason must be more careful. When his helicopter finally emerges from its house he gives it a single task: to take a mother and her child home after school. They meet no monsters and the child does not get lost. It is as safe a game as nighttime–morning time. That game, though he did not invent it, was similarly well designed for Jason. The instant he perceived the logic of its limits, his gratitude was boundless. No matter who joined the play, the pattern remained the same.

I must not allow the simplicity of a nighttime–morning time game to mask its underlying themes of fear and delivery. Nor can I avoid the implications of all the locked up, trapped, chained, jailed, and lost characters that occupy the thoughts of our young dramatists. What is the essential fear, then? What or who is really doing the locking up, and what does the lost child search for?

Jason may be revealing the biggest piece of the story. In his fantasy play no one has arrived to take the schoolchild home; *the child is lost at school.* Jason's helicopter will be the agent of rescue, from school to home. The ultimate fear and loss, Jason tells us, is separation.

If he is right, then aside from all else we try to accomplish, we have an awesome responsibility. We must become aware of the essential loneliness of each child. Our classrooms, at all levels, must look more like happy families and secure homes, the kind in which all family members can tell their private stories, knowing they will be listened to with affection and respect.

As always, I end the school year with more questions than answers. Jason, alone in his helicopter house, has become for me the symbol of Every Child's sense of being alone and misunderstood in the classroom. We all know that we are unique; no one else is exactly like you or me. The key that unlocks each one of us is somewhere out there. Who will find it?

New Questions

"Are you going to ask good questions or bad questions?"

"Which are the bad ones, Joseph?"

"Like if someone took something or if they did a bad thing."

"What kind do you like?"

"The good kind. The pretty kind."

I have just retold "The Three Pigs," at Joseph's request, and he surprises me. Joseph is seldom loath to demolish a happy ending, and his own play and stories are riddled with bad characters. Yet he worries now about my questions. Has he picked up the uncertainties I have about fairy tales?

Samantha agrees with Joseph. "He means not the wicked kind. And Jason either doesn't like that, do you, Jason?"

Jason shakes his head, but it is a fact that the first time he ever entered a formal discussion the issue could well have been of the "bad" kind: Did the mother pig know there was a wolf in the forest?

"I'm not sure I know which questions are bad, Joseph. Last week, when I asked if the queen should have given her baby to Rumpelstiltskin since she'd promised to, was that a bad question?"

"Bad, bad, bad."

"Even though everyone wanted to answer it? You all agreed she was right to keep the baby."

"Because she was used to it already," Arlene says, repeating her original response.

"And I remember, Joseph, you said that Rumpelstiltskin shouldn't have even asked for the baby, that it was a bad thing to do."

"It *was* a bad thing, so that's why it's a bad question."

"Oh, I see. Well, as it happens, there's no time for questions and, besides, we've already had two 'Three Pigs' discussions."

"'Member I said how she could trick the wolf?"

"I do. Joseph said the mother wanted her children to escape before the wolf came. By the way, when I asked if the mother pig missed her children, was that good or bad?"

"That really was good, Joseph," Samantha decides. "Because she really does miss them."

Gail and Trish are as curious as I am about bad questions. "Is it a new category?" Gail asks.

"Well, she didn't call the question bad," Trish remembers, "but Arlene did not want to be asked about the monster in her 'What's the matter, baby?' story. In fact, didn't the monster have to stand outside the stage?"

"Right. The story wasn't supposed to be about the dream. Maybe fairy tales remind children of their bad dreams."

"Or do they *give* them bad dreams?" Gail wonders. "Babies given away, stepmothers who don't like their children . . ."

"Little pigs alone in the forest, bad wolves and such."

"By the way, Vivian, speaking of questions, we've been noticing something. You're still the one who asks most of the fairy tale questions, do you realize? The children ask about every other sort of book and, of course, they question each other during storytelling, but in fairy tales . . ."

"Don't I usually say, 'After I tell this fairy tale, I have a question for you?' I don't say that when I read a regular picture book. Oh, and also, I'm *telling* the story, not reading it. Is that a factor?"

My assistants' observations are confirmed the following day. When Edward dictates a story, he is quizzed so often by Eli, there is nothing for me to ask.

"Then comed the enemy," Edward says, "and the enemy fighted the dragon."

"Do enemies fight dragons?" Eli asks.

Edward ignores the implication of Eli's question. "Then Superman is there and he killed the enemy."

Eli is more explicit. "Is the dragon good?"

"Yeah, because I'm the dragon," Edward explains.

"When I grow up I'm being a dragon for a while," Edward decides, "then a astronaut."

Edward listens with interest to Eli's comments, then continues his story. "I need a dad and a mother in my story and a baby and a babysitter. And a father."

"A dad *is* a father," Eli corrects him.

"This is a different father. Not the dragon. That's you, Eli. We're good dragons, everyone is good in our family."

When we act out the story, my role is also limited, to that of reader. Those chosen to be dragons ask all the questions— mainly about whether dragons, like witches, are inherently bad. Yet there seems to be no such thing as a bad question, not even "Am I bleeding?" from Joseph, as he lays dying.

Later, when I tell "Jack and the Beanstalk," I am uncomfortably aware of my role as principal question asker, but I am even more conscious of the kind of questions the children do ask: Will my narration follow the "real" events of the story? They take for granted that fairy tales have the power to frighten them.

In Edward's dragon story, there is no "real" way; everything is open to negotiations. But fairy tales seem to have a life of their own, no matter how the sympathetic adult attempts to shield the listener.

"Will the giant eat Jack?" Samantha asks, despite her familiarity with the plot.

"No, Jack escapes easily."

"Good. I forgotted if the real way had that."

Did she really forget? Or is it that she remembers only too well those hidden messages that burst out unexpectedly in fairy tales.

"Then they heard the giant coming," I continue, leaving out "Fee, fie, fo, fum."

"Does the giant see him?"

"No, he's hiding, but he can peek at the giant. And when the giant falls asleep counting his gold, Jack grabs two bags to bring to his mother and they're never poor again and . . ."

"The giant has to chase Jack," Edward says.

"I know, but I promised this wouldn't be scary. Now, let me think of a question you'll like. Meanwhile, maybe someone wants to say something about Jack? Or about the giant?"

The children seem too preoccupied to speak. After several moments of quietness, they begin to tumble against one another and, quickly, I offer my preplanned question.

"Why was the giant's wife so nice to Jack, I wonder."

"Womens are nice," Alex responds, coming to a halt at my feet. "They like little boys."

Everyone is suddenly attentive, anticipating my next question. They expect the "Jack" questions to come from me, as if I alone possess the "real" questions. They feel stirred up and need to hear their thoughts transposed into words, and hear also what their friends are thinking.

"I wonder if the giant's wife had a little boy of her own," I say. Is this a good or bad question?

"She used to," Samantha states emphatically. "But the giant eated him by mistake. He didn't know that was his child."

Is this what Samantha thinks? She warns me not to scare her and then devises an event more terrible than any in the original rendition. Did my question suggest the idea to her? More likely, she imagined the possibility of mistaken identity at some previous hearing of the story, and my question enabled her to reveal the thought. Or, do I rationalize in order to continue drawing upon fairy tales for good discussion material?

"You're right, Samantha!" Joseph shouts. "And then the lady thought Jack is her son that was ate up because it was a long time ago and she didn't remember what he looked like."

"He weared different clothes," Simon adds, giving further supportive evidence.

"Or he was a girl," Jason whispers.

"And when he comed alive again he went to live with the

poor woman because she was lonely and didn't have a cat," Arlene decides.

"Or a girl baby," Jason repeats.

"The giant ate up the girl baby," Alex tells him, "and also the father." The group quietly contemplates the series of tragedies set before them, none of which came from me or from the fairy tale.

If given enough time, the children will take all my questions, good and bad, to the same place: the fate of a vulnerable child surrounded by uncertainty and danger. They caution me about fairy tales, but there is an avalanche of excited responses whenever we discuss them—as if the children have been waiting for someone to unlock the gates to their dreams. I remember Joseph's front and back gates to the dream. When a fairy tale is told or read, that wicked lion Joseph imagined must be pushing at the "white part" trying to enter.

If the children so distrust the "real" way, it must be that the reality of every magical tale includes their own hidden anxieties and extended images. But, if this is so, then to be questioned in ways that allow one to embellish, explain, fend off, judge, or deny might be good. Can't bad questions lead to good answers?

"This is becoming a real dilemma for me," I say, after school. "Maybe these children are too young for fairy tales."

Gail nods sympathetically. "Or, maybe we should tell the stories as written, since everyone expects the worst anyway."

"Well, it *is* sort of a game, the way I do it. I tell a euphemistic version of a story the children remember in its original form, and then we discuss a hypothetical series of events that are more moral and more terrible than mine or the book's. But I'm certain that this is the way the children want to proceed. They won't let me tell it the real way; they are even more insistent that we cannot act it out the real way. But, when the subject is open for discussion, there are no limits. They are absolutely fearless."

"You know, you're right," Trish says. "Samantha doesn't want *you* to mention the giant's child-eating habits, but if she or another child bring up the matter, it's okay."

"Which carries me back to my dilemma: Shall we tell fairy tales or not?"

"Maybe it's different when a child hears these stories at home, on mommy's lap," Gail muses.

"That's a good point," I tell her. "In school they've just entered the forest themselves. By the way, remember when Jason was Jack for a few moments, in the doll corner? Then he reversed his direction immediately and grew smaller and smaller? See, that's the intuitive way to handle all this fairy tale information. Even Jason knew how to protect himself, without being told what to do."

"So, are you saying, just tell the fairy tales but don't talk about them? Let the children play them out in their own ways?"

"Or rewrite them in their own stories," I add. "Look at what Edward did with Cinderella yesterday. 'The stepmother did not like Cinderella. Then came the prince and he killed the dragon.' Now, what if I'd asked, 'Why doesn't the stepmother like Cinderella?'"

"That would have been one of Joseph's bad questions, for sure."

"Probably. But would Edward, in a discussion, have been able to change the stepmother into a dragon and have the prince kill her? He gets rid of the bad feelings engendered by the stepmother not by talking about them but by slaying a dragon and . . ."

"But wait, Vivian," Trish interrupts. "Had you posed that question to the group and Edward heard other opinions and rationalizations, it might have served as useful a purpose as slaying a dragon. I mean, maybe both approaches are necessary."

I seem to have borrowed a page from Jason's "determined ambivalence" period. Fairy tales yes, fairy tales no. I am on the verge of stopping them for this age group, but a colleague who teaches first grade wants to attend one of these discussions and has already arranged for some time off. I choose "Goldilocks and the Three Bears" as a fairly mild story, thinking I'll tell it in its original form.

However, the moment I say, "She knocked on the door and nobody answered," Samantha jumps up.

"I don't want to listen," she whines.

Joseph follows suit. "I hate this story."

"I won't say anything scary, I promise."

"Are you going to make the bears happy to see her? Or the real way?"

"Will the father bear yell at her?" This question is from Edward.

"Well, I thought I'd have them sort of surprised. But I'll make them happy if you wish, and no yelling."

"Are you sure?"

"Arlene, don't I always change a story if someone asks me to? That's why I tell these stories instead of reading them."

"Did you in 'The Three Pigs'?"

"Sure. Nobody was eaten, not even the wolf."

"But, in the real way," Arlene states, "the wolf does eat two pigs, right?"

"Do you think about the real way even when I make changes?"

Arlene doesn't reply, but I see how complex the subject is. "The Three Pigs" is not *Hot Hippo* in which the central question seems to concern freedom of choice: Can Hippo decide for himself whether to live on land or in the water? Can Alex sit next to Joseph whenever he wishes? Can Jason fly uninvited into Simon's story?

Perhaps these issues appear so urgent because they are substitutes for the real thing. The fairy tales, in one way or another, hit squarely at the single most important issue for any child: Will I be abandoned? Will it happen to me as it does to the pigs? How will I recognize when it's about to occur? What can I do to forestall the inevitable?

I continue the story. "The little bear said, 'I don't mind if she's in my bed. I want to play with her. May I?'"

"Is he pretending? Wake her up gently," Lilly urges. It seems there is no way to erase the picture of a lost child in a strange house.

Yet, once the discussion begins, the children are eager to announce their ideas. Hands are waving, eyes are shining, and I too am carried away by the joy of communal discourse on serious matters.

Teacher:	Why did Goldilocks decide to go in?
Arlene:	She didn't know whose house it is.
Joseph:	She couldn't tell who lives there if it's a bear or not.
Jason:	The bears do live there.
Samantha:	Maybe she thought it was her own house.
Teacher:	Can someone make such a mistake?
Alex:	Sure. Probably it looked like the same house that's hers.
Arlene:	She was curious of what was inside.
Eli:	The porridge was there.
Teacher:	Was she wise to eat it?
Everyone:	No! No!
Teacher:	I suppose she was hungry.
Arlene:	She should of just seed what was in there and said, well, when I get home I'll ask my mom to make me some porridge.
Katie:	No, she doesn't tell her mom 'cause her mom said don't go.
Lilly:	She wanted to go for a nap. That's why she came in.
Teacher:	Oh, she was tired.
Edward:	Let her sleep on the floor.
Simon:	On the grass she should.
Katie:	Grass is too cold.
Arlene:	I got a sleeping bag. It's very soft for that.

Teacher:	So you think she shouldn't have slept in the bear's bed.
Samantha:	In your own bed is where. Or in mommy's bed.
Joseph:	My mom lets me when daddy's on a trip.
Lilly:	When I have a bad dream I can.
Teacher:	Maybe Goldilocks can do that when she has a bad dream.

The children think about mommy's bed and are not pleased by a careless girl who sleeps in strange beds. I assure them that Goldilocks smiles at baby bear, but the children feel the terror in her heart. Samantha must rewrite the story, practicing avoidance as I do.

> Goldilocks saw the bears' house and she ran home.
> Then her mother played with her all day and she
> doesn't go to work.

Yet, at other times, Samantha exaggerates the danger. I remember her story in which the three pigs are eaten, first by the big bad wolf and then "they got ate up by all the big bad wolfs."

Joseph also retells the Goldilocks story and, though he has been known to have her eaten or put in a dungeon, this time he too sidesteps the issue of her safety in the bears' house.

> The three bears. And a wolf was there. He blowed
> their house down.

Lilly understands his intentions. "When Goldilocks goes by there she doesn't see a house?" I wouldn't have known enough to ask that question.

"She saw a different house," Joseph replies. "Her own house."

This idea makes good emotional sense to Lilly. No one at the story table rejects Joseph's theory, and I refrain from asking bad questions, such as: Was she lost in the forest? Is that why she suddenly found her own house?

It seems I can ask Lilly any number of questions about her own lost girls, and I can subject Joseph's wolves, lions, and wicked alligators to intense scrutiny at any time without disturbing the children's mood of confidence, but I never know in advance when a reference to the "real" Goldilocks will stir up the deep waters.

My own deepest feelings have been agitated by the fairy tale issue. The material is guaranteed to excite the sort of extensive disclosure that enriches discussions, storytelling, and play itself. Furthermore, upon entering the children's fantasies, these ideas are quickly transformed into controllable forms. Unlike the rest of us, children are able to invent new stories instantly to dispel unwelcome images.

But is it wise or necessary for the teacher to be the messenger of disturbing thoughts? Joseph's bad-good distinction forces me to face the issue because he is a boy whose play and stories continually ask and answer their own risky questions within a safe, limited context.

Fairy tales must create the sort of trap Jason has spent half a year trying to avoid: that bottomless stream of "accidental" connections. Are the fairy tales, for the class, equivalent to the squirrel hole for Jason? It seemed dangerous at first, but after many encounters and trial entrances, the squirrel hole proved to be just the place to test and expand the helicopter fantasy. If this is the case, then I ought to tell fairy tales *more* often. Unless, of course, the absence of novelty begins to encourage ritualistic responses.

"Why struggle with all of this?" Trish asks me. "Since you have all these doubts. Why not just give up the fairy tales for now?"

"I guess I'm not ready to do that yet. Every day there are stories like Edward's yesterday that turn fairy tale themes into useful social documents." Edward hardly entered "The Three

Bears" discussion but, in his story, he deals with two of its primary issues.

> Once upon a time it was Edward in a big dark for-
> est. Then a bear came. Joseph and Katie and Simon
> came. A bad bear.

He objects when I return his story to the pile after we act it out. "I didn't finish. I need more people to come in the forest with me."

"Who else will come with Edward?" I ask.

Arlene raises her hand. "What do we do when we see the bear?"

"Shoot him and lock him up."

"Then I won't be the bear," Alex says. "Only if I come alive and eat my porridge."

"Yeah, you could. It cooled off for you."

Edward will not walk alone in the forest and the bear still has the comfort of his porridge. These immediate problems are solved, but I have more questions in my mind.

Would Edward even be in the forest without such tales as "The Three Bears"? Perhaps not. But he could use the other dark places he knows: behind the stairs, under the bed, in the hallway. He needn't be in the forest, though somehow a forest seems the perfect setting in which to imagine being alone and afraid.

Didn't our discussion also help Edward deal with feelings of loneliness? He could picture Goldilocks in a cozy sleeping bag, having just discovered that the bears' house is exactly like her own where her mother awaits with a bowl of porridge. And perhaps, if she has a bad dream about the bears, she can crawl into mommy's bed. All of these ideas are now Edward's to use in play and storytelling but, most important, to reflect upon each time he hears "The Three Bears."

Certainly he will hear the story often. By four, the children have been exposed to a wide variety of fairy tale plots in books, cartoons, and film. As with most scenarios, children seem to assume that the more frightening story is the "real" way, a concept that fits the universal expectation of tragedy once we are old enough to experience and fantasize the fear of abandonment.

Fantasy, of course, is the first line of defense against every sort of fear, and, in fantasy play, the children discover the value of peer support as they dare to put the beanstalk and forest to the test. Gradually their private protective symbols blend with communal rituals to build semblances of safe retreats in the outside world.

"This is the bears' house," Lilly tells Jason.

"Are you Goldilocks?"

"I'm the mother bear. We're not having Goldilocks. You want to be baby bear?"

"I'm the brother."

"No helicopter, okay?"

"Yeah, you could have one in the forest not by the trees. Is there a wolf?"

"No wolf."

Play sets up its straw men and knocks them down quickly, too fast to see beneath the subterfuge. Real questions are changed into pretend questions, and the original issue disappears into the forest or is swallowed up in the hum of helicopter blades.

Moreover, when the subject is play, the teacher's questions deal mostly with disguises and seldom with what lies underneath. The storytelling format is often more revealing, but here too there is a natural protective device at work that prevents self-incrimination.

Lilly's families often do little besides eat, sleep, and brush their teeth. Joseph and Simon sleep in squirrel holes, but, in a discussion of "The Three Bears," we are told how good it is to sleep in mommy's bed when one is frightened. The fairy tale itself must be a euphemism for the deeper, darker fears that already exist.

Then why not allow children to handle such matters in childlike ways, through play and storytelling of their own making? These are, after all, the children's natural, intuitive means for interpreting all aspects of their world. Putting aside the fact that fairy tales cannot be avoided, why are they needed?

Perhaps because they are such good stories. They represent the adult version of childhood fantasy, presented in a cohesive, theatrical style that is perfectly suited to the endemic thinking of children. Not the least of the fairy tale's superior power lies in its obvious connection to mankind's original fantasies as represented in the play of young children.

How odd it seems: Joseph decides there are good and bad questions and, suddenly, the whole fairy tale issue comes alive for me. I am sharply reminded of how much exists beneath the surface of every encounter I record and describe.

Have I given sufficient attention to those thoughts that cannot be put into play and storytelling? Do I search for new ways to help each child unlock and open up the gates to full participation in classroom life?

I end the year with Joseph's enigma and Jason's determined ambivalence. What they recognize intuitively, I must subject to further scrutiny with my tape recorder and in my journals. Perhaps it is a new beginning in my ongoing analysis of teaching: What are the good and bad questions? How does each kind free the spirit and release the hidden words?

Joseph's view of the nature of questioning ignites my curiosity. We both know that even better than the growl of the lion, the cry of a baby, and the roar of a helicopter is the *word*, spoken aloud for all to hear. If Joseph's question draws me into new ways of hearing the words spoken in my classroom, then it makes sense to begin by studying the children's questions. How else can I find out what "good" and "bad" mean?